GoodFood

101 CUPCAKES & SMALL BAKES
TRIPLE-TESTED RECIPES

Editor
Jane Hornby

BOOKS

Contents

Introduction

It's no wonder we've re-kindled our love affair with batch-baking. Small bakes are easy to make, fun to share and warm the heart.

Fluffy, frosted New-York-style cupcakes are in all the shops these days – but home-made will always taste best, fresh from the cooling rack. Our Easy chocolate cupcakes, page 10, are rich but light, and ready in under an hour.

The 1990s brought a coffee shop to every corner, and with them came light and fruity muffins. Our Classic blueberry muffin, page 62, is a brilliant basic and can be adapted to whatever fruit is in season. Or, if you're more 'tea for two' than 'skinny latté', whip up a plate of scones instead – Easy fluffy scones on page 46 are a great place to start.

Biscuit-lovers have a lot to look forward to with such treats as melt-in-the-mouth shortbread and crumbly cookies. Bars and slices range from indulgent chocolate numbers to more sustaining granola bars and flapjacks – and I haven't even started on the selection of dead-easy tray bakes and small pastries, pies and tarts that complete this cute collection.

The icing on the cake? Every recipe has been triple-tested by us here at *Good Food* magazine to work first time for you.

Jane Hornby
Good Food magazine

Notes and conversion tables

NOTES ON THE RECIPES

• Eggs are large in the UK and Australia and extra large in America unless stated otherwise.

• Wash fresh produce before preparation.

• Recipes contain nutritional analyses for 'sugar', which means the total sugar content including all natural sugars in the ingredients, unless otherwise stated.

OVEN TEMPERATURES

Gas	°C	°C Fan	°F	Oven temp.
¼	110	90	225	Very cool
½	120	100	250	Very cool
1	140	120	275	Cool or slow
2	150	130	300	Cool or slow
3	160	140	325	Warm
4	180	160	350	Moderate
5	190	170	375	Moderately hot
6	200	180	400	Fairly hot
7	220	200	425	Hot
8	230	210	450	Very hot
9	240	220	475	Very hot

APPROXIMATE WEIGHT CONVERSIONS

• All the recipes in this book list both imperial and metric measurements. Conversions are approximate and have been rounded up or down. Follow one set of measurements only; do not mix the two.

• Cup measurements, which are used by cooks in Australia and America, have not been listed here as they vary from ingredient to ingredient. Kitchen scales should be used to measure dry/solid ingredients.

Good Food are concerned about sustainable sourcing and animal welfare so where possible, we use organic ingredients, humanely-reared meats, free-range chickens and eggs and unrefined sugar.

SPOON MEASURES

Spoon measurements are level unless otherwise specified.

- 1 teaspoon (tsp) = 5ml
- 1 tablespoon (tbsp) = 15ml
- 1 Australian tablespoon = 20ml (cooks in Australia should measure 3 teaspoons where 1 tablespoon is specified in a recipe)

APPROXIMATE LIQUID CONVERSIONS

metric	imperial	AUS	US
50ml	2fl oz	¼ cup	¼ cup
125ml	4fl oz	½ cup	½ cup
175ml	6fl oz	¾ cup	¾ cup
225ml	8fl oz	1 cup	1 cup
300ml	10fl oz/½ pint	½ pint	1¼ cups
450ml	16fl oz	2 cups	2 cups/1 pint
600ml	20fl oz/1 pint	1 pint	2½ cups
1 litre	35fl oz/1¾ pints	1¾ pints	1 quart

These light cakes are perfect for freezing before icing – they just need a quick blast in the microwave to bring them back to life.

Easy chocolate cupcakes

300g/10oz dark chocolate, broken into chunks (you don't need to use one with a high cocoa content)
200g/8oz self-raising flour
200g/8oz light muscovado sugar, plus 3 tbsp extra
6 tbsp cocoa powder
150ml/¼ pint sunflower oil, plus a little extra for greasing
284ml pot soured cream
2 large eggs
1 tsp vanilla extract

Takes 35 minutes, plus cooling
Makes 10

1 Preheat the oven to 180°C/160°C fan/gas 4 and line 10 holes of a 12-hole muffin tin with paper cases. Whiz the chocolate into small pieces in a food processor.

2 Take a large mixing bowl and tip in the flour, sugar, cocoa, oil, 100ml/3½fl oz of the soured cream, the eggs, vanilla and 100ml/3½fl oz of water. Whisk everything together with electric beaters until smooth, then quickly stir in 100g/4oz of the whizzed-up chocolate bits. Divide among the cases, then bake for 20 minutes until a skewer inserted comes out clean (make sure you don't poke it into a chocolate-chip bit). Cool on a wire rack.

3 To make the icing, put the remaining chocolate, soured cream and 3 tablespoons of sugar in a small pan. Heat gently, stirring, until the chocolate is melted and you have a smooth icing. Chill in the fridge until firm enough to swirl on top of the cakes, then tuck in.

• Per cake 534 kcalories, protein 6g, carbohydrate 62g, fat 31g, saturated fat 11g, fibre 2g, sugar 46g, salt 0.3g

Get creative over Easter and make some special cupcakes.
Either buy sugared almonds to decorate, or shape your own
pastel-coloured eggs using bought marzipan.

Simnel egg cupcakes

100g/4oz butter, softened
100g/4oz golden caster sugar
2 large eggs
100g/4oz self-raising flour, plus
1 level tbsp
1 tsp baking powder
1 tsp finely grated orange zest
25g/1oz ground almonds

TO DECORATE
home-made marzipan, to make eggs
edible paste food colours (we used
claret, baby blue and primrose
yellow)
200g/8oz fondant icing sugar
shimmery hundreds and thousands
and sugared almonds, to scatter

Takes 55 minutes, plus cooling
Makes 12

1 Preheat the oven to 180°C/160°C fan/
gas 4. Line a muffin tin with 12 paper cases.
Beat together the butter, sugar, eggs, flour,
baking powder and orange zest until smooth
and creamy, then fold in the almonds.
2 Spoon the mix into the cases then bake
for 20 minutes or until risen and golden and
firm to the touch. Cool on a wire rack.
3 To make the marzipan eggs, colour
some white marzipan with food colouring
then shape into eggs. For the icing, mix the
icing sugar with 2 tablespoons of water until
smooth. Divide among three small bowls and
colour one with the claret, one with baby blue
and one yellow. Spoon the icing over the
cakes and drizzle over the eggs, if you like.
Leave to set then scatter with a few hundreds
and thousands and a sugared almond or
marzipan egg.

• Per cake 242 kcalories, protein 4g, carbohydrate 34g,
fat 11g, saturated fat 5g, fibre 1g, sugar 27g, salt 0.4g

Cheesecake meets cake in these adorable little bakes
that are ideal for tea or as a dessert.

Blueberry lemon cakes with cheesecake topping

100g/4oz butter, softened, plus extra
for greasing
100g/4oz golden caster sugar
2 large eggs, lightly beaten
zest and juice of 1 lemon
140g/5oz self-raising flour
50g/2oz blueberries

FOR THE TOPPING
250ml/9fl oz soured cream
25g/1oz icing sugar
1 large egg
1 tsp vanilla extract

Takes 35 minutes, plus cooling
Makes 12

1 Butter a 12-hole muffin tin. Cross over two 1.5cm strips of baking parchment in each hole – they need to stick up a bit from the tin as you'll use them as handles to remove the cakes when they are cooked.
2 Preheat the oven to 180°C/160°C fan/gas 4. Beat together the butter and sugar until pale. Gradually beat in the eggs, then mix in the lemon zest and juice and fold in the flour.
3 Divide among the muffin holes, smooth the tops then sprinkle a few blueberries over each cake, reserving the rest for later. Bake for 12 minutes then remove from the oven.
4 Whisk the topping ingredients together until smooth. Gently press down the tops, then spoon the topping over each cake. Scatter with the remaining blueberries and bake for 5–7 minutes more.

• Per cake 252 kcalories, protein 3g, carbohydrate 21g, fat 18g, saturated fat 10g, fibre none, sugar 12g, salt 0.32g

The beauty of these little cakes is in their simplicity – a little icing sugar and a sugar flower turn a basic fairy cake into a chic little something.

Glamorous fairy cakes

140g/5oz butter, very well softened
140g/5oz golden caster sugar
3 medium eggs
100g/4oz self-raising flour
25g/1oz custard powder or cornflour

TO DECORATE
600g/1lb 5oz icing sugar, sifted
6 tbsp water
green and pink food colourings
crystallized violets, roses or rose petals
edible wafer flowers

Takes 30 minutes, plus cooling
Makes 24

1 Preheat the oven to 190°C/fan 170°C/gas 5 and arrange paper cases in two 12-hole bun tins. Put all the cake ingredients in a large bowl and beat for about 2 minutes until smooth. Divide the mixture among the cases so they are half filled and bake for 12–15 minutes, until risen and golden. Cool on a wire rack.
2 Mix the icing sugar and water, and use to top eight cakes. Split the remaining icing and colour it with pink and green colouring. Use to top the remaining cakes then finish each cake with a flower or petal.

• Per cake 193 kcalories, protein 2g, carbohydrate 36g, fat 6g, saturated fat 3g, fibre none, added sugar 31g, salt 0.2g

Get creepy in the kitchen at Halloween with these clever cakes, just the thing for trick-or-treaters or a Halloween party.

Spooky spider cakes

200g/8oz butter, at room temperature
200g/8oz golden caster sugar
200g/8oz self-raising flour
4 large eggs
½ tsp baking powder
1 tsp vanilla extract
6 tbsp chocolate chips or chopped chocolate

TO DECORATE
2 packs liquorice Catherine wheels
12 tbsp chocolate-nut spread
Liquorice Allsorts (the black ones with the white centre)
1 length red bootlace
1 tube black writing icing

Takes 1 hour, plus cooling • Makes 12

1 Preheat the oven to 180°C/160°C fan/gas 4 and line a 12-hole muffin tin with paper cases, preferably brown ones. For the cake, beat everything but the chocolate together until smooth. Stir in the chocolate. Spoon into the cases then bake for 20–25 minutes until golden and risen. Cool on a wire rack.

2 Unravel the liquorice wheels and cut into lengths to make dangly legs. Stick eight into each cake, making small cuts in the sponge with the tip of a sharp knife so they push in really securely.

3 Spoon the chocolate spread on top and spread lightly to make a round spider's body. Now cut the Allsorts to make eyes and the red bootlace to make mouths, then stick them on to the cakes and dot on the icing to make eyeballs. Will keep for up to 2 days in a cool place.

• Per cake 481 kcalories, protein 6g, carbohydrate 63g, fat 24g, saturated fat 10g, fibre 1g, sugar 45g, salt 0.64g

Add plenty of wow to your Christmas table with these easy chocolate and cherry puds – ideal for those not keen on classic fruit cake.

Christmas pud cupcakes

140g/5oz butter, plus extra for greasing
50g/2oz dark chocolate, broken into chunks
100ml/3½fl oz soured cream
3 large eggs, lightly beaten
140g/5oz self-raising flour
140g/5oz golden caster sugar
100g/4oz ground almonds
6 tbsp cocoa powder
1 tsp baking powder
85g/3oz dried sour cherries, plus a few extra to decorate

TO DECORATE
250g/9oz icing sugar, sifted
1 tsp custard powder, sifted
12 small bay leaves

Takes about 40 minutes, plus cooling
Makes 12

1 Preheat the oven to 190°C/170°C fan/gas 5. Put a 12-hole silicone muffin tray on a baking sheet or butter a non-stick 12-hole muffin tin and stick two criss-crossing strips of baking parchment in each hole.
2 Melt the butter and chocolate together over a low heat. Cool, then stir in the soured cream and eggs. Mix the flour, sugar, almonds, cocoa and baking powders in a bowl. Pour in the chocolate mix and cherries, and stir until smooth. Spoon into the muffin holes, then bake for 20 minutes. Cool in the tins for 5 minutes, then remove to a wire rack.
3 Mix the icing sugar and custard powder with 2 tablespoons of water to make a thick icing. Cut off any rounded muffin-tops, stand upside-down on the wire cooling rack, then spoon over the icing. Leave to set, then top with the bay leaves and the remaining cherries. Best eaten on the day.

• Per cake 413 kcalories, protein 6g, carbohydrate 54g, fat 20g, saturated fat 10g, fibre 2g, sugar 42g, salt 0.51g

Just the thing with a coffee on a Saturday morning,
these cakes are simple to make and sure to please.

Mini coffee cakes

100g/4oz walnut halves
140g/5oz unsalted butter, softened
140g/5oz caster sugar
3 large eggs, beaten
1 tsp vanilla extract
3 tbsp strong coffee (espresso or made with instant), cooled
175g/6oz plain flour
4 tsp baking powder

FOR THE ICING
85g/3oz unsalted butter, softened
140g/5oz icing sugar

Takes 45–50 minutes, plus cooling
Makes 12

1 Preheat the oven to 180°C/160°C fan/ gas 4 and line a 12-hole muffin tin with paper cases. Finely chop all but twelve of the walnut halves.
2 Beat the butter and sugar together until pale, then gradually beat in the eggs. Add the chopped walnuts, vanilla and 2 tablespoons of the coffee. Mix the flour and baking powder, fold in gently, then divide the mix among the baking cases. Bake for 15–20 minutes until golden. Cool on a wire rack.
3 To make the icing, beat together the butter and sugar and remaining coffee. Ice the cooled cakes, then decorate with nuts.

• Per cake 387 kcalories, protein 5g, carbohydrate 37g, fat 25g, saturated fat 11g, fibre 1g, sugar 25g, salt 0.57g

Don't just save these for Christmas – they're a fabulous
storecupboard-friendly cake that everyone will love
(and taste great with custard as a quick pud, too).

Little mince pie cakes

175g/6oz self-raising flour
100g/4oz light muscovado sugar
1 tsp mixed spice
175g/6oz butter, softened
3 large eggs
2 tbsp milk
about 140g/5oz mincemeat
icing sugar, for dusting

Takes 40 minutes, plus cooling
Makes 12

1 Preheat the oven to 190°C/170°C fan/
gas 5. Line a 12-hole muffin tin with paper
cases. Put the flour, sugar, spice, butter,
eggs and milk into a mixing bowl, and beat
with an electric hand whisk or wooden spoon
for around 2–3 minutes until the mix is light
and fluffy.
2 Put a spoonful of cake mix in each
paper case, then a rounded teaspoon of
mincemeat. Cover the mincemeat with a
spoonful of cake mix and smooth.
3 Bake for 15–18 minutes until golden brown
and firm. Dust with icing sugar and serve
warm or cold.

• Per cake 272 kcalories, protein 4g, carbohydrate
33g, fat 15g, saturated fat 9g, fibre 1g, added sugar
19g, salt 0.4g

A great marriage of two sweet classics, these will disappear in no time.

Doughnut cupcakes

200g/8oz softened butter, plus
3 tbsp melted
200g/8oz golden caster sugar
2 large eggs, plus 1 yolk
300g/10oz self-raising flour
100ml/3½fl oz milk
½ tsp baking powder
12 tsp strawberry jam (about ⅓ of a
regular jar)
3–4 sugar cubes, roughly crushed

Takes 40 minutes, plus cooling
Makes 12

1 Preheat the oven to 180°C/160°C fan/
gas 4. Line a 12-hole muffin tin with paper
cases. Tip the softened butter, sugar, eggs,
flour, milk and baking powder into a large
bowl. Beat together just until you have a
smooth, soft batter.
2 Fill the cases two-thirds full with the batter,
then make a small dip in the top of each one
and spoon in 1 teaspoon of jam. Cover with
another tablespoon of cake batter. Bake for
25 minutes until risen and cooked through.
Cool on a wire rack.
3 Brush some melted butter over each cake,
then simply sprinkle with the crushed sugar
and serve. Will keep for up to 2 days in an
airtight container.

• Per cake 363 kcalories, protein 4g, carbohydrate
47g, fat 19g, saturated fat 11g, fibre 1g, sugar 28g,
salt 0.66g

Soft vanilla cupcakes topped with a snowy, mallow frosting are the ultimate treat for Christmas or any other celebration.

Snow-capped fairy cakes

175g/6oz butter
175g/6oz golden caster sugar
3 large eggs
200g/8oz self-raising flour
zest of 1 orange
1 tsp vanilla extract
4 tbsp milk

FOR THE FROSTING
1 egg white
4 tbsp fresh orange juice
175g/6oz icing sugar
edible gold and silver balls and thinly sliced fruit jellies, to decorate

Takes 35 minutes, plus cooling
Makes 18

1 Preheat the oven to 190°C/170°C fan/ gas 5. Line 18 holes of two 12-hole muffin tins with paper cases. Melt the butter and cool for 5 minutes, then tip into a large bowl with all the cake ingredients. Beat together until smooth.
2 Spoon the cake mixture into the cake cases, filling them three-quarters full. Bake for 15–18 minutes until lightly browned and firm to the touch. Cool on a wire rack.
3 To make the frosting, put the egg white and orange juice into a heatproof bowl, sift in the icing sugar, then set over a pan of simmering water. Using an electric hand whisk, whisk the icing for 7 minutes until it is glossy and stands in soft peaks. Whisk for a further 2 minutes off the heat.
4 Swirl the frosting on to the cakes, then decorate with fruit jellies and a few silver balls. Leave to set.

• Per cake 211 kcalories, protein 3g, carbohydrate 31g, fat 9g, saturated fat 5g, fibre none, sugar 22g, salt 0.31g

Who could resist a pretty pile of these fruity cupcakes?

Raspberry cupcakes with orange drizzle

200g/8oz self-raising flour
2 tsp baking powder
200g/8oz unsalted butter, softened
4 large eggs
200g/8oz caster sugar
3 tbsp milk
50g/2oz ground almonds
zest of 1 medium orange
150g punnet raspberries, lightly crushed, plus extra to decorate

FOR THE SUGAR CRUST
juice of 1 medium orange
4 tbsp caster sugar

Takes 35 minutes, plus cooling
Makes 12

1 Preheat the oven to 180°C/160°C fan/gas 4. Line a 12-hole muffin tin with paper cases. Tip the first eight ingredients into a large bowl and beat with an electric whisk until smooth. Fold the crushed raspberries through the batter.

2 Divide the batter among the cases (they should be about half full) and bake for around 20–25 minutes or until golden and just firm. Make the topping by mixing together the orange juice and sugar.

3 Remove the cupcakes from the oven and allow to cool a little. Put on to a wire rack then drizzle each with the orange and sugar crust mix. Top with the extra raspberries to decorate, then serve.

• Per cake 328 kcalories, protein 5g, carbohydrate 37g, fat 19g, saturated fat 10g, fibre 1g, sugar 25g, salt 0.44g

If you're cooking this recipe out of gooseberry season, frozen berries work just as well.

Gooseberry gems

225g/8½oz self-raising flour
1 tsp baking powder
200g/8oz golden caster sugar
3 large eggs
150g pot natural yogurt
4 tbsp elderflower cordial
175g/6oz butter, melted and cooled

FOR THE FOOL
350g/12oz gooseberries, topped and tailed, or use frozen
50g/2oz golden caster sugar
1 tbsp elderflower cordial
200ml pot crème fraîche
icing sugar, for dusting

Takes 30 minutes, plus cooling
Makes 12

1 Preheat the oven to 200°C/180°C fan/ gas 6. Line a 12-hole muffin tin with paper cases. Mix the dry ingredients together in a large bowl. Beat the eggs, yogurt, elderflower cordial and melted butter with a pinch of salt, then stir into the dry ingredients. Spoon into the cases, bake for 18–20 minutes until risen and golden, then cool on a wire rack.
2 Gently cook the gooseberries with the sugar in a pan for 10 minutes until the berries have collapsed a little. Stir in the cordial, taste and add more sugar, if you like, then cool. Fold into the crème fraîche.
3 To serve, cut a heart from the top of each cake using a small serrated knife or, if that's too fiddly, simply cut off the top and cut it in half, like a butterfly cake. Spoon a little fool into each cake, top with the piece that you cut away, then dust with a little icing sugar.

• Per cake 370 kcalories, protein 5g, carbohydrate 43g, fat 21g, saturated fat 13g, fibre 1g, sugar 29g, salt 0.61g

Using polenta and fresh strawberries makes these
little cakes especially light and fragrant.

Strawberry and polenta cupcakes

140g/5oz unsalted butter, softened
140g/5oz golden caster sugar
zest of ½ lemon
85g/3oz polenta
3 large eggs, beaten
140g/5oz plain flour
1 tsp baking powder
1 tbsp milk
140g/5oz strawberries, hulled and
chopped

TO DECORATE
3 strawberries, hulled and roughly
chopped, plus 6 halved
juice of 1 lemon
140g/5oz icing sugar, sifted

Takes 35 minutes, plus cooling
Makes 12

1 Line a 12-hole muffin tin with paper cases and preheat the oven to 180°C/160°C fan/ gas 4. Beat together the butter, sugar and lemon zest until pale. Beat in the polenta followed by the eggs, a little at a time.
2 Sift in the flour and baking powder, then fold in quickly with a large metal spoon. Fold in the milk and chopped strawberries. Spoon into the paper cases, then bake for around 20 minutes or until golden and risen. Cool on a wire rack.
3 Peel the cases from the cakes. For the icing, put the chopped strawberries in a bowl with 1 teaspoon of lemon juice and mash to a pulp. Sieve, then add the juice to the sugar to turn it pink. Stir in more lemon juice, drop by drop, to make a thick but flowing icing. Dip each cake into the icing, then top with a strawberry half. Leave to set, then serve.

• Per cake 271 kcalories, protein 4g, carbohydrate 40g, fat 12g, saturated fat 7g, fibre 1g, sugar 26g, salt 0.19g

Now here's a new use for that tin of custard powder at the back of the cupboard. The butter should be soft but not greasy for the best result.

Custard buns

100g/4oz custard powder
200g/8oz butter, softened a little
2 large eggs
4 tbsp milk
140g/5oz caster sugar
100g/4oz self-raising flour, sifted

FOR THE ICING
140g/5oz icing sugar
hundreds and thousands, to decorate

Takes 30 minutes, plus cooling
Makes 12

1 Preheat the oven to 180°C/160°C fan/gas 4 and line a 12-hole muffin tin with paper cases. Beat the custard powder with the butter, eggs and milk, then stir in the sugar and fold in the sifted flour. Spoon into the paper cases.
2 Bake for about 20 minutes until a skewer inserted into the centre comes out clean. Leave to cool completely.
3 For the icing, mix the icing sugar with about 3 tablespoons of water to form a thick paste. Cover the tops of the buns with the icing, then decorate straight away with hundreds and thousands.

• Per bun 299 kcalories, protein 2g, carbohydrate 40g, fat 15g, saturated fat 9g, fibre none, sugar 26g, salt 0.45g

These look really impressive but are simple to make. They'll take you back to toasting marshmallows around an open fire.

Campfire cupcakes

140g/5oz light muscovado sugar
100g/4oz self-raising flour
50g/2oz cocoa powder
1 tsp baking powder
3 large eggs
125ml/4fl oz vegetable oil
3 tbsp milk
50g/2oz milk chocolate chips
30g pack mini marshmallows

Takes 30 minutes, plus cooling
Makes 12

1 Preheat the oven to 180°C/160°C fan/ gas 4 and line a 12-hole muffin tin with paper cases. Tip the sugar, flour, cocoa and baking powders into a large bowl. Whisk together the eggs, oil and milk, then stir together with the dry ingredients until well combined. Add the milk chocolate chips.

2 Divide the mixture among the paper cases, then bake for 20 minutes until risen and cooked through. Leave to cool (you can now store them for up to 2 days in an airtight container).

3 Just before serving (either warm from the oven or cold), arrange marshmallows over the tops of the cakes. Heat the grill to medium and pop the cakes under it for 30 seconds, watching them all the time, or until the marshmallows are lightly browned. Remove and eat straight away.

• Per cake 233 kcalories, protein 3g, carbohydrate 25g, fat 14g, saturated fat 3g, fibre 1g, sugar 16g, salt 0.27g

If you've been asked to make cupcakes for a wedding or special occasion, try our moist and tasty vanilla and white-chocolate-topped cakes. They'll keep happily in a cool place for up to 48 hours.

Romantic rose cupcakes

150ml pot natural yogurt
3 large eggs, beaten
1 tsp vanilla extract
175g/6oz golden caster sugar
140g/5oz self-raising flour
1 tsp baking powder
100g/4oz ground almonds
a pinch of salt
175g/6oz unsalted butter, melted

TO DECORATE
100g/4oz white chocolate
140g/5oz unsalted butter
140g/5oz icing sugar
36 small sugar roses and leaves,
bought or home-made
2.5m thin pink ribbon (optional)

Takes 30 minutes, plus cooling and decorating • Makes 12

1 Line a 12-hole muffin tin with deep paper cases and preheat the oven to 190°C/170°C fan/gas 5. Mix the yogurt, eggs and vanilla in a jug. Mix the dry ingredients in a large bowl and make a well in the centre.
2 Add the wet mix and the butter to the bowl, then quickly fold in with a large metal spoon – don't overwork it. Fill the cases and bake for 18–20 minutes until golden and springy. Cool for 2 minutes then cool completely on a wire rack. Keep in an airtight container for up to 2 days or freeze as soon as possible.
3 For the frosting, melt the chocolate in the microwave on High for 1½ minutes, stirring halfway. Cool. Beat the icing sugar and butter until creamy. Beat in the chocolate. Spread over the cakes or chill and bring back to room temperature before using. Decorate with roses and tie or glue ribbon on, if you like. Keep them cool but don't chill.

• Per cake 525 kcalories, protein 6g, carbohydrate 57g, fat 32g, saturated fat 16g, fibre 1g, sugar 47g, salt 0.36g

As a modern twist to traditional fruit cake, these cupcakes make a great gift and would go down a storm at a Christmas bazaar. Will keep in an airtight tin for up to 3 weeks.

Christmas cupcakes

200g/8oz dark muscovado sugar
175g/6oz butter, chopped
700g/1lb 9oz luxury dried mixed fruit
50g/2oz glacé cherries
2 tsp freshly grated ginger
zest and juice 1 orange
100ml/3½oz dark rum, brandy
or fresh orange juice
85g/3oz pecan nuts, roughly chopped
3 large eggs, beaten
85g/3oz ground almonds
200g/8oz plain flour, sifted
½ tsp baking powder
1 tsp each mixed spice and cinnamon

TO DECORATE
500g pack ready-rolled marzipan
4 tbsp apricot jam, warmed
500g pack fondant icing sugar
sugared almonds and snowflake
sprinkles

Takes about 1½ hours, plus cooling
Makes 12

1 Tip the first seven ingredients into a pan. Slowly bring to the boil, stirring frequently. Reduce the heat and bubble gently for 10 minutes, stirring often. Cool for 30 minutes.
2 Preheat the oven to 150°C/130°C fan/gas 2 and line a 12-hole muffin tin with paper cases. Stir the nuts, eggs and ground almonds into the fruit then add the flour, baking powder and spices. Once evenly mixed, scoop into the cases and level the tops with a wet spoon. Bake for 35–45 minutes, until an inserted skewer comes out clean.
3 Dust the work surface with a little icing sugar then stamp out 6cm rounds from the marzipan. Brush the cooled cakes with jam, top with marzipan and press down lightly.
4 Make the fondant icing as per the packet instructions then spread over the cakes. Decorate with the sugared almonds and snowflakes.

• Per cake 751 kcalories, protein 9g, carbohydrate 119g, fat 28g, saturated fat 9g, fibre 3g, sugar 105g, salt 0.44g

Dark, milk and white chocolate melt together to make these muffins completely irresistible.

Triple-chocolate-chunk muffins

250g/9oz plain flour
25g/1oz cocoa powder
2 tsp baking powder
½ tsp bicarbonate of soda
85g/3oz each dark and white chocolate, broken into chunks
100g/4oz milk chocolate, broken into chunks
2 large eggs, beaten
284ml pot soured cream
85g/3oz light muscovado sugar
85g/3oz butter, melted

Takes 35 minutes, plus cooling
Makes 11

1 Preheat the oven to 200°C/180°C fan/gas 6. Butter eleven holes of a muffin tin. In a large bowl, combine the flour, cocoa and baking powders, bicarbonate of soda and all the chocolate chunks. In a separate bowl, mix together the eggs, soured cream, sugar and butter.
2 Add the soured-cream mixture to the flour mixture and stir until just combined and fairly stiff; don't overmix – the mixture should look quite lumpy. Spoon the mixture into the muffin tin to fill the holes generously.
3 Bake for 20 minutes until well risen. Leave to cool in the tin for about 15 minutes as the mixture is quite soft. Remove from the tin and cool on a wire rack. Eat while still warm and the chocolate is gooey.

• Per muffin 325 kcalories, protein 6g, carbohydrate 37g, fat 18g, saturated fat 11g, fibre 1g, added sugar 17g, salt 0.72g

These scones are the business – light but with a nice crusty outside, and ready in under 30 minutes. Add 85g/3oz sultanas or chopped glacé cherries in with the sugar, if you like.

Easy fluffy scones

350g/12oz self-raising flour, plus
more for dusting
½ tsp salt
1 tsp baking powder
85g/3oz cold butter, cut into cubes
4 tbsp golden caster sugar
150g pot natural full-fat yogurt
4 tbsp full-fat milk
1 tsp vanilla extract
1 egg beaten with 1 tbsp milk,
to glaze

Takes about 25 minutes • Makes 9

1 Preheat the oven to 220°C/200°C fan/gas 7 and put a baking sheet inside to heat. Put the flour, salt and baking powder into a food processor, and whiz in the butter until it disappears. Pulse in the sugar; tip it all into a large bowl, then make a well in the middle.
2 In a pan over a low heat, warm the yogurt, milk and vanilla together until hot (it may go a bit lumpy-looking). Pour it into the bowl and quickly work into the flour with a cutlery knife. Stop as soon as it's all in.
3 Tip the mix on to a floured surface and fold it over a few times to create a smooth-ish dough. Press out to about 4cm thick, then stamp out four 7cm diameter rounds. Squash the trimmings together then repeat. Brush the tops with egg glaze, scatter flour over the hot sheet, then add the scones. Bake for around 12 minutes until risen and golden.

• Per scone 233 kcalories, protein 5g, carbohydrate 36g, fat 9g, saturated fat 5g, fibre 1g, sugar 9g, salt 0.8g

Peaches and almonds get along famously, but normally in calorific cakes and pastries. These little muffins are low in fat and can be served warm as a pudding with a scoop of something creamy.

Peach and almond muffins

3 large eggs
100g/4oz golden caster sugar, plus a little extra for sprinkling
a few drops of almond extract
25g/1oz butter, melted
100g/4oz self-raising flour
25g/1oz ground almonds
2 tbsp peach conserve or apricot jam
2 small peaches, halved, stoned and sliced
1 tbsp flaked almonds
half-fat crème fraîche, to serve

Takes 35–40 minutes, plus cooling
Makes 6

1 Preheat the oven to 220°C/200°C fan/ gas 7. In a large bowl, use a hand whisk to mix the eggs, sugar and almond extract together for a minute until foamy. Pour in the melted butter and continue to beat until combined. Gently fold in the flour, ground almonds and a pinch of salt.
2 Divide the muffin mixture among six holes of a non-stick muffin tin. Top each with a blob of conserve or jam and arrange a few slices of peach on top. Scatter over the almonds and a little extra sugar, then bake for 20–25 minutes until puffed up and golden. Serve warm with a spoonful of half-fat crème fraîche, or leave to cool. Best eaten the day they're made or frozen while still slightly warm.

• Per muffin 245 kcalories, protein 7g, carbohydrate 34g, fat 10g, saturated fat 3g, fibre 1g, added sugar 17g, salt 0.34g

Adding sweet grated carrot and pineapple to muffins means that you don't need loads of sugar for this cute children's bake.

Rudolf's snowball carrot muffins

425g can pineapple in juice
200g/8oz self-raising flour
1 tsp bicarbonate of soda
85g/3oz golden caster sugar
50g/2oz desiccated coconut
2 large eggs
85g/3oz butter, melted
150g pot natural bio yogurt
175g/6oz grated carrot

TO DECORATE
50g creamed coconut sachet
juice from the pineapple can
100g/4oz icing sugar
50g/2oz desiccated coconut
orange writing icing
crystallized angelica

Takes 30 minutes, plus cooling
Makes 12

1 Preheat the oven to 200°C/180°C fan/ gas 6 and line a 12-hole muffin tin with paper cases. Drain the pineapple, reserve the juice, then crush the flesh with a fork.
2 Combine the dry ingredients in a large bowl. Beat the eggs, melted butter and yogurt together, and pour into the bowl with the grated carrot and crushed pineapple. Stir until just combined, then spoon into the cases. Bake for 18 minutes or until risen and golden.
3 Mix the creamed coconut with around 5 tablespoons of pineapple juice and stir in the icing sugar. Put the coconut on a plate. Peel the cooled muffins from their cases and put them on a wire rack. Spread the icing over until completely covered (this can get a bit messy), then roll them in the coconut. Dry for a few minutes. Pipe a carrot on the top of each muffin using the writing icing, and add strips of angelica as stalks.

• Per muffin 287 kcalories, protein 4g, carbohydrate 38g, fat 14g, saturated fat 10g, fibre 2g, sugar 25g, salt 0.63g

Everyone will love these muffins for breakfast.
They're gluten free but still light and fluffy.

Date and brown sugar muffins

50g/2oz butter, plus extra for greasing
50g/2oz dark brown soft sugar, plus extra for sprinkling
2 medium eggs
200ml/7fl oz buttermilk
100g/4oz quick-cook polenta or fine cornmeal
100g/4oz rice flour
1 rounded tsp baking powder (most are gluten free but check the pack)
50g/2oz dates, stoned and chopped

Takes 35 minutes • Makes 6

1 Preheat the oven to 200°C/180°C fan/gas 6. Butter six holes of a muffin tin. Beat together the butter and sugar until creamy. Beat in the eggs, one at a time, then stir in the buttermilk.

2 Mix the polenta or cornmeal, rice flour and baking powder in a bowl, then fold this into the other mixture. Add the dates.

3 Spoon into the tin and sprinkle with the extra sugar. Bake the muffins for 25–30 minutes until risen and golden.

• Per muffin 283 kcalories, protein 6g, carbohydrate 44g, fat 10g, saturated fat 6g, fibre 1g, added sugar 10g, salt 0.69g

Tempt the one you love with these wicked little chocolate cakes.

Chocolate heart muffins

250g/9oz plain flour
½ tsp bicarbonate of soda
2 tsp baking powder
100g/4oz caster sugar
100g/4oz butter
200g/8oz dark chocolate
250ml/9fl oz buttermilk
2 medium eggs
icing sugar, for dusting
chocolate hearts, to decorate,
optional

Takes 35 minutes, plus cooling
Makes 10

1 Preheat the oven to 200°C/180°C fan/ gas 6. Butter then flour 10 mini-heart baking tins (or 10 holes of a muffin tin).
2 Mix together the dry ingredients in a large bowl. Melt the butter and chocolate together in a pan over a gentle heat. Off the heat, beat in the buttermilk and eggs. Fold the wet ingredients into the dry, but try not to overmix.
3 Spoon the mix into the tins or muffin holes, then bake for 20–25 minutes, until risen and springy. Cool in the tin for 10 minutes, then ease out with a spatula and dust with icing sugar. Decorate with chocolate hearts, if you like.

• Per muffin 285 kcalories, protein 5g, carbohydrate 39g, fat 13g, saturated fat 8g, fibre 1g, sugar 23g, salt 0.51g

For a change from the norm, roll a simple scone base around autumnal apples and spice. Eat warm, with more butter if you dare.

Fruity spiced swirls

1 tsp ground cinnamon
1 tsp ground nutmeg
3 tbsp demerara sugar
4 tbsp soft butter
1 eating apple, peeled and finely chopped
85g/3oz raisins

FOR THE DOUGH
350g/12oz self-raising flour, plus more for dusting
½ tsp salt
1 tsp baking powder
85g/3oz cold butter, cut into cubes
4 tbsp golden caster sugar
150g pot full-fat natural yogurt
4 tbsp full-fat milk
1 tsp vanilla extract
1 egg beaten with 1 tbsp milk, to glaze

Takes 25 minutes • Makes 10

1 Preheat the oven to 220°C/200°C fan/gas 7 and put a baking sheet in to heat. Beat ½ teaspoon of each spice and 2 tablespoons of demerara into the butter, then stir in the fruit.
2 To make the dough, mix the remaining spices, the flour, salt and baking powder in a food processor, then whiz in the butter until it disappears. Pulse in the sugar, tip into a large bowl, then make a well in the middle.
3 Gently warm the yogurt, milk and vanilla together until hot (it may go a bit lumpy looking). Tip it into the well in the bowl and quickly work into the flour with a cutlery knife. As soon as it's all in, stop.
4 Roll the dough to about 40x30cm on a floured surface. Spread with the fruity butter, roll up from the long side, tucking the ends over neatly, then cut into 10 triangles. Brush with egg glaze and scatter over the remaining sugar. Bake on a floured sheet for 14 minutes.

• Per swirl 254 kcalories, protein 5g, carbohydrate 40g, fat 10g, saturated fat 6g, fibre 1g, sugar 17g, salt 0.71g

Full of good-for-you ingredients, these easy muffins would make a great breakfast or lunchbox filler.

Banana muffins with streusel topping

1 tbsp golden linseed
25g/1oz self-raising flour
15g/½oz butter, at room temperature
40g/1½oz demerara sugar
½ tsp ground cinnamon

FOR THE MUFFINS
100g/4oz plain wholemeal flour
25g/1oz soya flour
3 tbsp light muscovado sugar
2 tsp baking powder
1 large egg
50ml/2fl oz soya milk
50ml/2fl oz sunflower oil
2 medium-sized ripe bananas, roughly mashed

Takes 45 minutes, plus cooling
Makes 6

1 Preheat the oven to 200°C/180°C fan/ gas 6. Line six holes of a muffin tin with paper cases. For the topping, whiz the seeds in a food processor, or put them in a plastic bag and pound them with a rolling pin until crushed. Rub the flour into the butter until the mixture resembles breadcrumbs. Add the linseed, sugar, and cinnamon. Stir in 2 teaspoons of cold water and mix well to moisten.
2 To make the muffins, mix the flours, muscovado sugar and baking powder together in a bowl, and make a well in the centre. Beat the egg, soya milk, oil and mashed banana together, then tip into the well. Stir to combine – don't overmix.
3 Spoon into the muffin cases until they are two-thirds full, then sprinkle a little of the streusel mixture over the top. Bake for around 20–25 minutes or until risen and golden.

• Per muffin 295 kcalories, protein 6g, carbohydrate 39g, fat 14g, saturated fat 3g, fibre 3g, added sugar 15g, salt 0.63g

Spread with clotted cream, these scones make the easiest cream tea ever, and are perfect for a picnic too.

Raspberry scones

225g/8½oz self-raising flour
1 tsp baking powder
1 heaped tbsp caster sugar
50g/2oz butter, diced, plus extra for greasing
about 200ml/7fl oz buttermilk
100g/4oz raspberries
clotted cream, to serve

Takes 30–35 minutes, plus cooling
Makes 6

1 Preheat the oven to 220°C/200°C fan/gas 7 and butter a baking sheet. Sift the flour and baking powder into a bowl then stir in the sugar. Rub in the butter until the mixture resembles breadcrumbs.

2 Make a well in the centre then gradually add enough buttermilk to mix to a soft, but not sticky, dough. Toss in the raspberries and, using your hands, carefully push them into the dough. The fruit will break up a bit and the dough become streaked.

3 Divide the mixture into six, then plop these mounds on to the baking sheet. Bake for 12–14 minutes until golden brown and cooked through. Remove to a wire rack to cool, then tear apart and spread with clotted cream.

• Per scone 223 kcalories, protein 5g, carbohydrate 36g, fat 8g, saturated fat 5g, fibre 2g, added sugar 5g, salt 0.8g

An easy recipe for light, fluffy blueberry muffins every time.

Classic blueberry muffins

140g/5oz caster sugar
250g/9oz self-raising flour
1 tsp bicarbonate of soda
85g/3oz butter, melted and cooled
2 large eggs, beaten
200ml/7fl oz milk
1 tsp vanilla extract
150g punnet blueberries

Takes 30 minutes, plus cooling
Makes 12

1 Preheat the oven to 200°C/180°C fan/gas 6. Line a 12-hole muffin tin with paper cases. In a bowl, combine the dry ingredients. Mix the butter, eggs, milk and vanilla in a jug, pour into the flour mix then stir until just combined. Don't overmix or the muffins will be tough. Fold in the blueberries.
2 Spoon the mixture into the cases and bake for 15–18 minutes until golden and firm. Remove from the tin and cool on a wire rack.

• Per muffin 194 kcalories, protein 4g, carbohydrate 30g, fat 7g, saturated fat 4g, fibre 1g, added sugar 12g, salt 0.68g

Muffins are great to make with kids as the batter doesn't need to be perfectly smooth, and they're quick to create together. These tasty cheese muffins make a great change to lunchbox sarnies.

Welsh rarebit muffins

225g/8oz self-raising flour
50g/2oz plain flour
1 tsp baking powder
½ tsp bicarbonate of soda
¼ tsp salt
½ tsp mustard powder
100g/4oz strong Cheddar,
half grated, half cubed
6 tbsp vegetable oil
150g pot Greek yogurt
125ml/4fl oz milk
1 large egg
1 tbsp Worcestershire sauce

Takes 40 minutes, plus cooling
Makes 12

1 Preheat the oven to 200°C/180°C fan/ gas 6. Line a 12-hole muffin tin with paper cases. Mix together the self-raising and plain flours, baking powder, bicarbonate of soda, salt and mustard powder in a bowl.
2 In another bowl, mix the cheese, oil, yogurt, milk, egg and Worcestershire sauce. Combine all the ingredients and divide among the muffin cases. Cook for 20–25 minutes until golden. Remove and cool slightly on a wire rack. Enjoy warm or cold.

• Per muffin 189 kcalories, protein 6g, carbohydrate 19g, fat 11g, saturated fat 4g, fibre 1g, sugar 1g, salt 0.79g

This is a clever twist on a traditional recipe. Ricotta makes
the scones lovely and moist, and the orange zest gives a
nice citrus kick to the flavour.

Crunchy-crusted citrus scones

175g/6oz ricotta
finely grated zest of 1 orange
100g/4oz golden caster sugar
200g/8oz self-raising flour, plus extra
for sprinkling
50g/2oz butter, cubed, plus extra
for greasing
1–2 tbsp milk, plus extra for brushing
1 tbsp demerara sugar
cream or butter and lemon or orange
curd, to serve

Takes 20–25 minutes, plus cooling
Makes 6

1 Preheat the oven to 200°C/180°C fan/
gas 6 and grease a baking sheet. Mix the
ricotta, orange zest and half the sugar until
combined. Sift the flour into another bowl and
add the remaining sugar. Rub the butter into
the flour mix so it looks like fine crumbs.
2 Stir the ricotta mix into the flour mix,
adding a tablespoon or two of milk to get a
soft (but not sticky) dough. Tip on to a floured
work surface and knead very lightly a few
times only. If you over-knead, the scones will
be tough. Roll or press the dough to a neat
round about 4cm thick. Place it on the baking
sheet and mark it into six wedges.
3 Brush with milk, sprinkle with a little flour
and the demerara. Bake for 20–25 minutes
until well risen and brown. Transfer to a wire
rack to cool slightly. Serve warm, with cream
or butter and lemon or orange curd.

• Per scone 299 kcalories, protein 6g, carbohydrate
48g, fat 11g, saturated fat 6g, fibre 1g, added sugar
20g, salt 0.39g

Just like a carrot cake, these muffins will keep beautifully moist.

Carrot and pineapple muffins

140g/5oz self-raising flour
85g/3oz wholemeal flour
½ tsp bicarbonate of soda
2 tsp ground cinnamon
150ml/¼ pint sunflower oil
100g/4oz golden caster sugar
200g/8oz mashed cooked carrot
3 canned pineapple slices,
cut into cubes
2 tbsp pineapple juice, from the can
1 large egg
1 tsp vanilla extract
50g/2oz sunflower seeds

Takes 30–35 minutes, plus cooling
Makes 12

1 Preheat the oven to 200°C/180°C fan/gas 6. Cut out a dozen 10cm squares of baking parchment and put them in a 12-hole muffin tin. Sift together the flours, reserving 2 tablespoons of the bran that collects in the sieve, then stir in the bicarbonate of soda, cinnamon and a pinch of salt.
2 In another bowl, beat the oil, sugar, carrot, pineapple cubes and juice, egg and vanilla. Stir the dry mix into the wet, then spoon into the tin. Sprinkle with the bran and a few sunflower seeds. Bake for 20–25 minutes or until an inserted skewer comes out clean. Leave to cool.

• Per muffin 239 kcalories, protein 4g, carbohydrate 26g, fat 14g, saturated fat 2g, fibre 2g, sugar 12g, salt 0.45g

Make a pot of coffee and enjoy a sweet muffin treat.

Raspberry coffee-time muffins

2 tbsp freshly ground coffee beans
100g/4oz butter
1 tbsp milk
400g/14oz self-raising flour
50g/2oz pine nuts, half of them toasted
175g/6oz golden caster sugar
1 tsp bicarbonate of soda
2 large eggs
284ml carton buttermilk or soured cream
200–250g/8–9oz fresh raspberries

Takes 45 minutes, plus cooling
Makes 12

1 Stir 2 tablespoons of boiling water into the coffee. Set aside for a few minutes. Preheat the oven to 200°C/180°C fan/gas 6. Cut out 12x10cm squares of baking parchment. Melt the butter, brush a little in each of the holes of a 12-hole muffin tin, then cool the rest slightly. Line the tin with the paper squares, so they stick up a bit. Strain the coffee and mix with the milk.

2 Mix the flour, toasted pine nuts, sugar and bicarbonate of soda in a large bowl. Beat the eggs, buttermilk or soured cream, cooled butter and coffee together. Stir into the flour mix until just combined. Tip in the raspberries, give a few more stirs, then spoon the mix into the tins. They'll be very full.

3 Scatter over the remaining pine nuts, then bake for 25 minutes or until risen and golden. Cool in the tin for a few minutes, then move to a wire cooling rack.

• Per muffin 287 kcalories, protein 6g, carbohydrate 43g, fat 11g, saturated fat 5g, fibre 2g, sugar 18g, salt 0.74g

New flavours in an old favourite – great for coffee mornings or an afternoon snack.

Mediterranean scones

350g/12oz self-raising flour, plus extra for dusting
1 tbsp baking powder
¼ tsp salt
50g/2oz butter, cut into pieces, plus extra for greasing
1 tbsp olive oil
8 Italian sun-dried tomato halves, coarsely chopped
100g/4oz feta, cubed
10 black olives, pitted and halved
300ml/½ pint full-fat milk
1 egg, beaten, to glaze

Takes 30–40 minutes, plus cooling
Makes 8

1 Preheat the oven to 220°C/200°C fan/gas 7. Butter a large baking sheet. In a large bowl, mix together the flour, baking powder and salt. Rub in the butter and oil until the mixture resembles fine breadcrumbs, then add the tomatoes, feta and olives. Make a well in the centre, pour in the milk and mix with a knife, using a cutting movement, until it becomes a soft 'stickyish' dough. Don't overhandle the dough.
2 Flour your hands and the work surface well, then shape the dough into a round, about 3–4cm thick. Cut into eight wedges and put them well apart on the baking sheet. Brush with beaten egg and then bake for 15–20 minutes until risen and golden. Transfer to a wire rack and cover with a clean tea towel as they cool to keep them soft. These are best served warm and buttered.

• Per scone 293 kcalories, protein 8g, carbohydrate 36g, fat 14g, saturated fat 7g, fibre 2g, added sugar none, salt 2g

These gooey muffins are delicious warm when the toffee is still melty,
or you can leave them to go cold and give them a quick reheat
in the microwave – about 20 seconds.

Pear and toffee muffins

300g/10oz self-raising flour
1 tsp baking powder
2 tsp ground cinnamon
85g/3oz golden caster sugar
250ml/9fl oz milk
2 large eggs, beaten
100g/4oz butter, melted
2 ripe pears, peeled, cored and cut
into small chunks
100g/4oz soft toffees, chopped
into pieces
25g/1oz flaked almonds

Takes 35–40 minutes, plus cooling
Makes 12

1 Preheat the oven to 200°C/180°C fan/
gas 6. Line a 12-hole muffin tin with
paper cases. Tip the flour, baking powder,
cinnamon and a pinch of salt into a large
bowl, then stir in the sugar. Mix together the
milk, eggs and melted butter in a large jug,
and pour into the dry mix all at once, along
with the pears and a third of the toffee. Stir
briefly until just beginning to combine to a
lumpy, streaky batter.
2 Spoon the mixture into the cases, then
sprinkle with the remaining toffee and the
flaked almonds. Bake for 25–30 minutes
until the muffins are risen, golden and feel
firm when pressed (the molten toffee will be
extremely hot so be careful not to touch it).
Remove from the tin to a wire rack to cool.

• Per muffin 257 kcalories, protein 5g, carbohydrate
36g, fat 11g, saturated fat 6g, fibre 1g, sugar 15g,
salt 0.62g

Make these if you've got kids over for a tea party –
they'll disappear in minutes (the muffins, not the kids).
Just be prepared for sticky fingers.

Cherry coconut muffins

100g/4oz butter, softened
100g/4oz golden caster sugar
2 large eggs, beaten
175g/6oz self-raising flour
5 tbsp milk
½ tsp vanilla extract
2 tbsp desiccated coconut
100g/4oz glacé cherries, cut into quarters

TO DECORATE
85g/3oz seedless raspberry jam
50g/2oz glacé cherries, cut into quarters
2 tbsp toasted desiccated coconut

Takes 35–45 minutes, plus cooling
Makes 9

1 Preheat the oven to 180°C/160°C fan/ gas 4. Line a muffin tin with nine paper cases. Beat the butter and sugar until pale and creamy, then beat in the eggs gradually until fluffy. Fold in the flour, milk, vanilla and coconut until you have a soft dropping consistency. Stir in the cherries.
2 Spoon the mixture into the paper cases and bake for 20 minutes until risen and golden. Lift the muffins out of the tin and sit them on a wire rack to cool slightly.
3 To decorate, tip the jam into a small pan and gently warm, stirring, until melted and smooth. Generously brush the tops of the warm cakes with the jam, stick the quartered cherries on top and sprinkle with the toasted coconut. Serve on the day of making.

• Per muffin 313 kcalories, protein 4g, carbohydrate 45g, fat 14g, saturated fat 9g, fibre 1g, added sugar 23g, salt 0.27g

Split and spread the scrumptious savoury scones with butter
then top with whatever you like. Try ham and soft cheese
or avocado for starters...

Cheddar scones

200g/8oz self-raising flour, plus
extra for dusting
50g/2oz butter, at room temperature
25g/1oz porridge oats
85g/3oz grated Cheddar, plus extra
for topping (optional)
150ml/¼ pint milk, plus extra
if needed

TO SERVE
butter, plus a topping of your choice

Takes 25 minutes • Makes 12–15

1 Preheat the oven to 220°C/200°C fan/
gas 7. Put the flour in a large bowl, then rub
in the butter. Stir in the oats and cheese, then
the milk. If it feels like it might be too dry and
crumbly, add a touch more milk, then bring
together to make a soft dough.
2 Lightly dust the work surface with a little
flour. Roll out the dough no thinner than 2cm.
Using a 4cm plain cutter, firmly stamp out
the rounds – try not to twist the cutter as this
makes the scones rise unevenly. Re-roll the
trimmings and stamp out more.
3 Transfer to a non-stick baking sheet, dust
with a little more flour or grated cheese, then
bake for 12–15 minutes until well risen and
golden. Cool on a wire rack before serving.

• Per scone 130 kcalories, protein 4g, carbohydrate
15g, fat 6g, saturated fat 4g, fibre 1g, sugar 1g,
salt 0.36g

Celebrate late summer's blackberries with this homely scone to tear and share at teatime.

Blackberry scones with blackberry jelly & clotted cream

50g/2oz butter, cut into small pieces,
plus extra for greasing
225g/8½oz self-raising flour,
plus extra for dusting
25g/1oz golden caster sugar
100g/4oz blackberries
150g pot natural yogurt (not fat free)
4 tbsp milk
blackberry jelly and clotted cream,
to serve

Takes 35 minutes • Makes 6

1 Preheat the oven to 220°C/200°C fan/gas 7. Line a baking sheet with baking parchment and lightly butter it. Rub the flour and butter together to make rough crumbs. Stir in the sugar, then very gently toss in the blackberries.

2 Mix the yogurt and the milk, pour into a well in the flour mix then very briefly stir together with a round-bladed knife to a soft dough. Flour your hands, then gently gather the dough into a rough ball. Don't knead, or the berries will get too mushy.

3 Put on a lightly floured surface, then gently pat to an 18cm circle about 2cm thick. Transfer to the baking sheet, mark into six wedges, then dust with a little flour. Bake for 18–20 minutes until risen and golden. Break into wedges while warm then serve with the blackberry jelly and clotted cream.

• Per scone 237 kcalories, protein 5g, carbohydrate 37g, fat 9g, saturated fat 5g, fibre 2g, sugar 8g, salt 0.55g

If you like American-style cookies, you'll love these pale, chewy delights, studded with cherry bits plus white and dark choc chips. Try swapping the glacé cherries for sour cherries or nuts.

Gooey chocolate cherry cookies

200g/8oz unsalted butter,
at room temperature
85g/3oz light muscovado sugar
85g/3oz golden caster sugar
1 large egg
225g/8½ oz self-raising flour
50g/2oz dark chocolate, 70% cocoa,
roughly chopped
50g/2oz white chocolate,
roughly chopped
85g/3oz undyed glacé cherries,
roughly chopped

Takes 30 minutes, plus cooling
Makes 20

1 Preheat the oven to 190°C/170°C fan/ gas 5. Beat the butter, sugars and egg until smooth, then mix in the flour, chocolates and cherry pieces and ½ teaspoon of salt. Spoon on to baking sheets lined with baking parchment in large rough blobs – you'll get twenty out of this mix. Make sure they are well spaced as the cookies grow substantially as they bake. The raw dough can be frozen.
2 Bake for 12–14 minutes until just golden but still quite pale and soft in the middle. If baking from frozen, give them a few minutes more. Cool on the sheets for 5 minutes, then lift on to wire racks with a fish slice and leave to cool completely.

• Per cookie 186 kcalories, protein 2g, carbohydrate 23g, fat 11g, saturated fat 6g, fibre 1g, sugar 14g, salt 0.13g

Hidden inside these crumbly biscuits lies a heart of lemon curd, giving an unexpected burst of flavour. If you're short of time though, leave out the lemon curd and just roll and stamp out lemony shortbreads.

Almond and lemon curd buttons

250g/9oz butter, softened
140g/5oz golden caster sugar, plus extra for sprinkling
1 large egg
1 tsp vanilla extract
zest of 2 lemons
300g/10oz plain flour, plus extra for rolling out
100g/4oz ground almonds
a little milk, to brush and seal
about 3 tbsp lemon curd
flaked almonds, to scatter

Takes 30 minutes, plus chilling and cooling • Makes about 20

1 Preheat the oven to 190°C/170°C fan/gas 5. Beat the butter, sugar, egg, vanilla, zest and a pinch of salt in a large bowl until smooth, then fold in the flour and ground almonds. Shape into two rounds, flatten them, then wrap in cling film and chill for 30 minutes.
2 Roll out one piece of dough on a floured surface until just thicker than a £1 coin, then stamp out rounds with a 7cm cutter. Brush all over with milk, then spoon roughly 20p-sized blobs of lemon curd into the middle of half of the rounds.
3 Carefully lay the remaining rounds on top of the lemon curd, then gently press around the edges with your fingers to seal. Scatter with a little caster sugar and the flaked almonds. Bake for 15 minutes until light golden. Cool. Repeat the process with any remaining pastry.

• Per biscuit 225 kcalories, protein 3g, carbohydrate 22g, fat 15g, saturated fat 7g, fibre 1g, sugar 10g, salt 0.21g

These oat-filled biscuits will keep for ages in the freezer
and make a great pick-me-up after a long day.

Freezer biscuits

250g pack butter, softened
200g/8oz brown soft sugar
1 tsp vanilla extract
2 large eggs
200g/8oz self-raising flour
140g/5oz oats
50g/2oz chopped nuts (try pecan
nuts, hazelnuts or almonds)
50g/2oz desiccated coconut
50g/2oz raisins or mixed fruit

Takes 30 minutes, plus cooling
Makes about 30

1 Beat the butter and sugar, then beat
in the vanilla and the eggs, one at a time.
Stir in a pinch of salt, the flour and oats to
make a stiff dough. Add the nuts, coconut
and dried fruit, and stir through.

2 Tear off an A4-sized sheet of greaseproof
paper. Spoon half the mix along the middle
of the sheet, then pull over one edge of
paper and roll up until you get a tight cylinder.
Roll until smooth. Twist up the ends, then
freeze for up to 3 months. Repeat with the
remaining mix.

3 When ready to cook, preheat the oven
to 180°C/160°C fan/gas 4 and unwrap the
frozen biscuit mix. Using a sharp knife, cut off
rounds roughly ½cm wide. If you have difficulty
slicing through, dip the knife into a cup of hot
water. Space widely apart on a baking sheet,
then bake for 15 minutes until golden brown.

• Per biscuit 138 kcalories, protein 2g, carbohydrate
16g, fat 8g, saturated fat 5g, fibre 1g, sugar 8g,
salt 0.21g

These craggy biscuits have a delicious melt-in-the-mouth texture. Store in an airtight container for up to 3 days, if you can resist them for that long!

Pistachio, orange and oat crumbles

a little oil, for greasing
125g/4½oz unsalted butter
125g/4½oz caster sugar
1 medium egg
2 tsp vanilla extract
125g/4½oz jumbo porridge oats
75g/2½oz plain flour
½ tsp baking powder
100g/4oz shelled pistachio nuts, roughly chopped
125g/4½oz orange-flavoured dark chocolate, cut into chunks

Takes 35 minutes, plus cooling
Makes 16

1 Preheat the oven to 180°C/160°C fan/ gas 4. Lightly oil two baking sheets. Beat the butter and sugar together in a large bowl until creamy. Beat in the egg, vanilla extract, oats, flour and baking powder until well combined. Stir in the pistachio nuts and chocolate chunks, and mix well.

2 Divide the mixture into 16 and spoon, spaced well apart, on to the baking sheets. Press down slightly with the back of a fork and bake for 15–20 minutes until golden. Allow to cool slightly before transferring to a wire rack to cool completely.

• Per biscuit 221 kcalories, protein 3g, carbohydrate 24g, fat 13g, saturated fat 6g, fibre 1g, sugar 13g, salt 0.07g

Try making these as a variation on cornflake cakes – perfect as a gift for the kids to make.

Storecupboard-friendly Florentines

85g/3oz cornflakes, bashed with a rolling pin to crush a bit
85g/3oz toasted flaked almonds
50g/2oz dried cranberries
50g/2oz glacé cherries, sliced thinly into rounds
397g can condensed milk
140g/5oz milk chocolate, broken into chunks
140g/5oz white chocolate, broken into chunks

Takes 25 minutes, plus cooling
Makes about 25

1 Preheat the oven to 180°C/160°C fan/ gas 4 and line a couple of baking sheets with baking parchment. Tip the crushed cornflakes, almonds, cranberries and cherries into a large bowl, then stir in the condensed milk until all the ingredients are sticky.
2 Spoon about 25 tablespoons of the mixture on to the sheets, and leave lots of room for spreading. Flatten each slightly with the back of a wet spoon and bake for 8–12 minutes until golden brown. Cool on the sheets for about 5 minutes, then carefully turn them upside down and transfer to another sheet of parchment to cool completely.
3 When cool, melt both the chocolates in a bowl set over a pan of simmering water or in the microwave. Spoon or brush the chocolate over the bases of the biscuits with a pastry brush. Leave to set, then serve or box up as presents.

• Per Florentine 158 kcalories, protein 3g, carbohydrate 21g, fat 7g, saturated fat 3g, fibre none, sugar 18g, salt 0.17g

Lebkuchen are traditional German biscuits, especially popular around Christmas time. They're similar to gingerbread in taste, but with a slightly chewy middle.

Lebkuchen

250g/9oz plain flour
85g/3oz ground almonds
2 tsp ground ginger
1 tsp ground cinnamon
1 tsp baking powder
½ tsp bicarbonate of soda
a pinch each of ground cloves, freshly grated nutmeg and ground black pepper
200ml/7fl oz clear honey
85g/3oz butter
zest of 1 lemon

FOR THE ICING
100g/4oz icing sugar
1 egg white, beaten

Takes 30 minutes, plus cooling
Makes about 30

1 Tip the dry ingredients into a large bowl. Heat the honey and butter in a pan over a low heat until the butter melts, then pour into the flour mixture along with the lemon zest. Mix well until the dough is combined and fairly solid. Cover and leave to cool.

2 Preheat the oven to 180°C/160°C fan/ gas 4. Using your hands, roll the dough into about 30 balls, each 3cm wide, then flatten each one slightly into a disc. Divide the biscuits between two baking sheets lined with baking parchment, spacing well apart. Bake for 15 minutes, then cool on a wire rack.

3 To ice the biscuits, mix together the icing sugar, egg white and 1–2 tablespoons of water to form a smooth, runny icing. Dip the top of each biscuit in the icing and spread with the back of a knife. Leave to dry out in a warm place. Store in an airtight container for up to a week.

• Per biscuit 102 kcalories, protein 2g, carbohydrate 16g, fat 4g, saturated fat 2g, fibre 0.5g, added sugar 9g, salt 0.16g

Bonfire night is the perfect excuse to try our special chewy cookies.
Once you've tried one batch, you'll be baking them all year round.

Toffee apple cookies

175g/6oz unsalted butter,
at room temperature
140g/5oz golden caster sugar
2 large egg yolks
50g/2oz ground almonds
85g/3oz chewy toffees,
roughly chopped
85g/3oz ready-to-eat dried apple
chunks, roughly chopped
225g/8½oz self-raising flour
2 tbsp milk

Takes 35–45 minutes • Makes about 24

1 Preheat the oven to 190°C/170°C fan/
gas 5. Using an electric whisk, beat together
the butter and sugar until pale and creamy.
2 Stir in the egg yolks, ground almonds,
toffees, dried apple and flour. Mix well
together then roll out into about 24 or so
walnut-sized balls.
3 Put well apart on two non-stick or lined
baking sheets and flatten the balls slightly
with your hand. Brush with milk then bake for
8–12 minutes until golden. Leave to firm up
for 5 minutes, then transfer to a wire rack and
allow to cool completely.

• Per cookie 148 kcalories, protein 2g, carbohydrate
17g, fat 8g, saturated fat 5g, fibre 1g, added sugar 7g,
salt 0.12g

Kids will love to help sandwiching these biscuits
with the melted marshmallow.

Jammy coconut mallows

250g/9oz butter, softened
140g/5oz golden caster sugar
1 large egg
1 tsp vanilla extract
300g/10oz plain flour
100g/4oz desiccated coconut

FOR THE MIDDLE AND COATING
about 175g/6oz raspberry jam
18 large marshmallows, cut in half
across the middle
25g/1oz desiccated coconut

Takes 50 minutes, plus chilling
and cooling • Makes 36

1 Preheat the oven to 190°C/170°C fan/
gas 5. Beat the butter, sugar, egg and vanilla
together with a pinch of salt until smooth. Fold
in the flour and coconut to form a dough.
2 On a floured surface, shape the dough
into a round, then roll to the thickness of a
£1 coin. Cut into eighteen rounds using a
6cm cutter. Lift onto baking sheets, then
bake for 14 minutes or until light golden. Cool
for 2 minutes, then transfer to a wire rack.
3 To sandwich the biscuits, lay half on a
baking sheet, under-side up. Put ½ teaspoon
of jam on each one, top with a marshmallow
half, then bake for 2 minutes until just melted.
Quickly top with the remaining biscuits,
pressing down so the marshmallow sticks
them together and oozes out a bit. Cool for
10 minutes. Put the coconut and remaining
jam on to plates, dip the edges in the jam,
then roll them in the coconut.

• Per mallow 140 kcalories, protein 1g, carbohydrate 16g,
fat 8g, saturated fat 6g, fibre 1g, sugar 10g, salt 0.12g

A little marmalade gives these simple cookies a subtle tang.

Marmalade and oat cookies

200g/8oz butter
175g/6oz brown soft sugar
2 tbsp thin-cut marmalade
2 tsp ground mixed spice
1 tsp ground cinnamon
1 tsp ground ginger
175g/6oz porridge oats
200g/8oz self-raising flour, plus
extra for dusting
2 tsp baking powder
175g/6oz dried fruit, try chopped
glacé cherries, apricots
and sultanas
100g/4oz nuts, chopped
(we used hazelnuts)

Takes 40 minutes • Makes about 20

1 Preheat the oven to 160°C/140°C fan/ gas 3 and line two baking sheets with parchment. Beat together the butter and sugar until light and fluffy. Mix the marmalade together with 2 tablespoons of boiling water. Stir into the creamed mix, then add the spices, oats, flour and baking powder. Mix in the fruit and nuts.

2 Dust your hands and the work surface with flour and roll the dough into a long sausage shape. Cut into about 20 discs. Put on the sheets, spacing them out well as they will spread. Bake for about 25 minutes until golden brown.

• Per cookie 236 kcalories, protein 4g, carbohydrate 30g, fat 12g, saturated fat 6g, fibre 2g, sugar 16g, salt 0.42g

You'll make a token effort to leave these on the tree,
but they won't stay there for long!

Orange and ginger
stained-glass biscuits

sunflower oil, for greasing
175g/6oz plain flour, plus
extra to dust
1 tsp ground ginger
zest of 1 orange
100g/4oz butter, cold, cut
into chunks
50g/2oz golden caster sugar
1 tbsp milk
12 fruit-flavoured boiled sweets
about 120cm thin ribbon, to decorate
icing sugar, to dust

Takes 35 minutes, plus chilling
and cooling • Makes 14

1 Preheat the oven to 180°C/160°C fan/
gas 4. Grease two large non-stick baking
sheets with oil. Whiz the flour, ginger, orange
zest and butter with 1 teaspoon of salt to fine
crumbs in a processor. Pulse in the sugar
and milk, then turn out and knead briefly until
smooth. Wrap, then chill for 30 minutes.
2 Roll the dough to the thickness of a £1
coin on a floured surface. Cut shapes with
7cm cutters, then use 4cm cutters to cut out
the middles. Make a hole in the top of each
biscuit, then lift them on to the baking sheets.
3 Crush the sweets with a rolling pin, then
put the pieces into the middles of the biscuits
– they should be level with the top of the
dough. Bake for 15–20 minutes or until golden
brown and the middles have melted. Leave
to harden, then transfer to a wire rack to cool.
Thread some ribbon through the hole in the
top of each biscuit, then dust with icing sugar.

• Per serving 160 kcalories, protein 2g, carbohydrate 23g,
fat 8g, saturated fat 5g, fibre 1g, sugar 10g, salt 0.14g

Italians love their biscotti – dipped into coffee or vin santo, a sweet dessert wine. Making your own is simple and really satisfying.

Fruity biscotti

350g/12oz plain flour, plus
extra for dusting
2 tsp baking powder
2 tsp ground mixed spice
250g/9oz golden caster sugar
3 large eggs, beaten
coarsely grated zest of 1 orange
85g/3oz raisins
85g/3oz dried cherries
50g/2oz blanched almonds
50g/2oz shelled pistachio nuts

Takes 1¼ hours, plus cooling
Makes about 72

1 Preheat the oven to 180°C/160°C fan/ gas 4. Line two baking sheets with baking parchment. Mix the flour, baking powder, spice and sugar in a large bowl. Stir in the eggs and orange zest, then bring together with your hands. Add the fruit and nuts, then work them in well.
2 Split the dough into four. With floured hands, roll into sausages 30cm long. Place on to the baking sheets. Bake for 25–30 minutes until the dough is pale but risen and firm. Cool for a few minutes. Meanwhile, turn down the oven to 140°C/120°C fan/gas 1.
3 Using a bread knife, cut the sausages diagonally into 1cm slices and then lay the slices flat on the baking sheets. Bake for around 15 minutes, turn over, then bake for another 15 minutes until dry and golden. Tip on to a wire rack to cool completely.

• Per biscuit 50 kcalories, protein 1g, carbohydrate 9g, fat 1g, saturated fat none, fibre none, sugar 6g, salt 0.06g

Kids will love to help you make these simple biscuits
that need just five storecupboard ingredients.

Simple jammy biscuits

200g/8oz self-raising flour
100g/4oz golden caster sugar
100g/4oz butter
1 large egg, lightly beaten
4 tbsp strawberry jam

Takes 20–25 minutes, plus cooling
Makes about 12

1 Preheat the oven to 190°C/170°C fan/ gas 5. Rub the flour, sugar and butter together until the mixture resembles breadcrumbs. Alternatively, you can do this in the food processor. Add enough egg to bring the mixture together to form a stiff dough.

2 Flour your hands and shape the dough into a cylinder, about 5cm across. Cut into finger-width slices and put on a large baking sheet. Space them out, as the mixture will spread when baking.

3 Make a small indentation in the middle of each biscuit with the end of a wooden spoon, then drop 1 teaspoon of jam into the centre. Bake for 10–15 minutes until slightly risen and just golden. Cool on a wire rack.

• Per biscuit 170 kcalories, protein 2g, carbohydrate 25g, fat 8g, saturated fat 5g, fibre 0.5g, sugar 13g, salt 0.3g

Make double the quantity of this fruity cookie dough and freeze it so that delicious home-baked biscuits are always close at hand.

Blueberry and pecan oaties

175g/6oz plain flour, plus extra for dusting
½ tsp baking powder
85g/3oz porridge oats
175g/6oz golden caster sugar
1 tsp ground cinnamon
140g/5oz cold butter, chopped
70g pack dried blueberries
50g/2oz pecan nuts, roughly broken
1 large egg, beaten

Takes 35 minutes, plus chilling and cooling • Makes 12

1 Tip the flour, baking powder, oats, sugar and cinnamon into a bowl, then mix well with your hands. Add the butter and rub into the mixture until it has disappeared. Stir in the blueberries and pecans, add the egg, then mix well with a cutlery knife or wooden spoon until it all comes together in a big ball. Lightly flour a work surface, then roll the dough into a fat sausage about 6cm across. Wrap in cling film, then chill in the fridge until solid.
2 Preheat the oven to 180°C/160°C fan/gas 4. Unwrap the dough and thickly slice into discs, and arrange on baking sheets. Bake for 15 minutes (or a few minutes more if you've frozen the sliced dough) until golden. Leave on the sheets to harden, then remove and cool completely on a wire rack before tucking in.

• Per biscuit 274 kcalories, protein 4g, carbohydrate 36g, fat 14g, saturated fat 7g, fibre 2g, sugar 20g, salt 0.27g

You can easily adapt this recipe to use raisins, sultanas or even chocolate chunks. Best eaten a day or two after baking.

Cranberry rockies

oil, for greasing
50g/2oz unsalted butter
100g/4oz self-raising flour
1 tsp ground mixed spice
50g/2oz light muscovado sugar
85g pack dried cranberries
1 small apple, halved, cored and finely diced
1 large egg, beaten
1 tbsp milk
icing sugar, to dust

Takes 35 minutes, plus cooling
Makes 8 large or 16 small

1 Preheat the oven to 180°C/160°C fan/ gas 4 and lightly oil a non-stick baking sheet. Rub together the butter and flour with your fingertips to fine breadcrumbs (or pulse in a food processor). Stir in the rest of the ingredients, except the icing sugar, until you have a soft dough.

2 Drop eight tablespoons or sixteen heaped teaspoons of the dough on to the baking sheet, spacing them out well. Bake for 18–20 minutes until golden. Transfer to a wire rack to cool, then dust with plenty of icing sugar. Pack into an airtight container or gift jars.

• Per cookie (16) 80 kcalories, protein 1g, carbohydrate 12g, fat 3g, saturated fat 2g, fibre 1g, added sugar 3g, salt 0.1g

You can't beat American-style cookies with big chunks
of chocolate and nuts. The perfect grown-up biscuit.

Chocolate-chunk pecan cookies

200g/8oz dark chocolate, 70%
cocoa solids, broken
into squares
100g/4oz butter, chopped
50g/2oz light muscovado sugar
85g/3oz golden caster sugar
1 tsp vanilla extract
1 large egg, beaten
100g/4oz whole pecan nuts
100g/4oz plain flour
1 tsp bicarbonate of soda

Takes 25 minutes, plus cooling
Makes 12

1 Preheat the oven to 180°C/160°C fan/
gas 4. Melt 85g/3oz of the chocolate in the
microwave on High for 1 minute or in a bowl
set over a pan of simmering water. Beat
in the butter, sugars, vanilla and egg until
smooth, then stir in three-quarters of both the
nuts and remaining chocolate, then the flour
and bicarbonate of soda.
2 Heap twelve spoonfuls, spaced apart,
on two baking sheets (don't spread the
mixture), then poke in the reserved nuts and
chocolate. Bake for 12 minutes until firm, then
leave to cool on the sheets. Can be stored in
an airtight container for up to 3 days.

• Per cookie 294 kcalories, protein 4g, carbohydrate
27g, fat 20g, saturated fat 8g, fibre 2g, sugar 17g,
salt 0.44g

Even the smallest hands can help to make
these friendly little fellows.

Double-ginger gingerbread men

140g/5oz unsalted butter
100g/4oz dark muscovado sugar
3 tbsp golden syrup
350g/12oz plain flour
1 tsp bicarbonate of soda
2 tsp ground ginger
1 tsp ground cinnamon
a pinch of cayenne pepper (optional)
2 balls stem ginger from a jar,
chopped

TO DECORATE
50g/2oz icing sugar
a few undyed glacé cherries,
halved then thinly sliced
2 balls stem ginger, cut into
small squares

Takes 30 minutes, plus cooling
Makes 12 large gingerbread men

1 Preheat the oven to 200°C/180°C fan/
gas 6. Line two baking sheets with baking
parchment. Melt the butter, sugar and syrup
in a pan. Mix the dry ingredients in a bowl
then stir in the butter mix and chopped ginger
to make a stiff-ish dough.
2 When cool, roll to about 5mm thick. Stamp
out gingerbread men, re-rolling the trimmings.
Lift on to the baking sheets and bake for
around 12 minutes until golden. Cool for
10 minutes, then lift on to wire cooling racks.
3 To decorate, mix icing sugar with a few
drops of water until thick and smooth. Spoon
the icing into a food bag, snip off just the
tiniest bit from one of the corners, then
squeeze buttons, eyes and a little smile on
to one man at a time. Stick on cherry smiles
and ginger buttons. Leave to set. Will keep
for up to 1 week in an airtight container.

• Per biscuit 262 kcalories, protein 3g, carbohydrate
43g, fat 10g, saturated fat 6g, fibre 1g, sugar 20g,
salt 0.27g

These freeze-ahead cookies are completely irresistible and a great recipe to make as gifts or for a cake sale.

Macadamia and cranberry American cookies

3 × 200g white chocolate bars, chopped
200g/8oz butter
2 large eggs
100g/4oz light muscovado sugar
175g/6oz golden caster sugar
2 tsp vanilla extract
350g/12oz plain flour
2 tsp baking powder
1 tsp ground cinnamon
100g/4oz dried cranberries
100g/4oz macadamia nuts, chopped

Takes 1 hour 10 minutes for 4–5 batches, plus cooling
Makes about 60

1 Preheat the oven to 180°C/160°C fan/gas 4. Melt 175g/6oz of the chocolate, then cool. Beat in the butter, eggs, sugars and vanilla, preferably with an electric hand whisk, until creamy. Stir in the flour, baking powder, cinnamon, cranberries, macadamias and 300g/10oz chopped chocolate.

2 Drop twelve small mounds on to a large baking sheet, spacing them well apart, then poke in some of the remaining chocolate, nuts and berries. Freeze now (see step 3) or bake for 12 minutes until pale golden. Leave to harden for 1–2 minutes, then cool on a wire rack. Repeat with the remaining dough.

3 Freeze raw cookie-dough scoops on baking sheets. When solid, pack them into a freezer container, interleaving the layers with baking parchment. Use within 3 months. Bake from frozen for 15–20 minutes.

• Per cookie 149 kcalories, protein 2g, carbohydrate 18g, fat 8g, saturated fat 4g, fibre none, sugar 13g, salt 0.14g

The refreshing flavour of Lady Grey tea, with its delicate infusions of orange, lemon and bergamot, makes for truly sophisticated biscuits.

Lady Grey biscuits

140g/5oz butter, softened
100g/4oz light muscovado sugar
2 tbsp Lady Grey tea leaves
50g/2oz dark chocolate,
finely chopped
1 large egg, beaten
200g/8oz plain flour

FOR THE ICING
140g/5oz icing sugar
2 tbsp strained Lady Grey tea
(strongly brewed)

Takes 35 minutes, plus chilling,
cooling and setting • Makes 40

1 Beat the butter and sugar until light and fluffy. Beat in the tea leaves, chocolate and egg, then fold in the flour to make a soft dough. Shape the dough into a sausage about 25cm/10in long, wrap tightly in cling film and chill for about 1 hour until firm.
2 Preheat the oven to 190°C/170°C fan/gas 5. Grease two baking sheets.
3 Cut slices off the roll of dough about 5mm/¼in thick. Place on the baking sheets, spacing them a little apart. Bake for 10–15 minutes until lightly browned, then cool on a rack.
4 Make the icing. Sift the sugar into a bowl, then beat in the tea until you have a smooth icing that is not too thick. Drizzle over each biscuit and leave to set.

• Per biscuit 77 kcalories, protein 0.9g, carbohydrate 11.1g, fat 3.5g, saturated fat 2.1g, fibre 0.2g, sugar 7g, salt 0.06g

Something sweet for those times when you need
a quick coffee and a burst of energy.

Fruit and nut squares
with chocolate drizzle

140g/5oz butter, plus extra
for greasing
200g/8oz porridge oats
25g/1oz desiccated coconut
50g/2oz light muscovado sugar
5 tbsp golden syrup
175g/6oz unsalted mixed nuts,
such as pistachio and peanuts,
chunkily chopped
50g/2oz dried cranberries or cherries
100g bar milk or dark chocolate

Takes 1 hour, plus cooling • Makes 12

1 Preheat the oven to 180°C/160°C fan/
gas 4. Butter an 18x28cm cake tin and line
the base with baking parchment. Mix together
the oats and coconut in a bowl. Melt the
butter in a pan over a medium heat with the
sugar and syrup. Give it an occasional stir
until the sugar has dissolved and the butter
has melted.
2 Off the heat, stir in the oat mix, nuts and
dried fruit. Leave until cold. Cut two-thirds of
the chocolate into chunks and stir into the
mix. Tip and spread the mixture into the tin.
Bake for 25–30 minutes until pale golden.
Mark into squares while still warm.
3 When completely cold, cut all the way
through. Melt the rest of the chocolate and
drizzle it over the bars. Will keep for a week
in an airtight container.

• Per square 345 kcalories, protein 6g, carbohydrate
29g, fat 24g, saturated fat 10g, fibre 3.1g, sugar 17g,
salt 0.25g

Halloween just got a little more gruesome! If you don't want to use nuts for the fingernails, you can use pieces of glacé cherry instead.

Freaky fingers

100g/4oz caster sugar
100g/4oz butter
1 large egg yolk
200g/8oz plain flour
½ tsp vanilla extract
20 blanched almonds
red food colouring, paste is best
(optional)

Takes 25 minutes, plus chilling
and cooling • Makes about 20

1 Line a baking sheet with parchment. Put the first five ingredients and a pinch of salt in a food processor, and whiz just until a ball of dough forms.
2 Tear off a golfball-sized piece of dough and use your hands to roll into a finger-sized cylinder. Repeat until you get about 20. Put the biscuits on to the sheet, well spaced apart.
3 Use a knife to make a few cuts, close together, for the knuckles. Put an almond at the end of each finger and trim away excess pastry around the edge. Chill for 30 minutes.
4 Meanwhile, preheat the oven to 190°C/ 170°C fan/gas 5. When chilled, bake for 10–12 minutes just until firm. Leave to cool a little, then paint the almonds with food colouring, if you like. Can be made up to 3 days ahead and stored in an airtight container.

• Per finger 102 kcalories, protein 1g, carbohydrate 13g, fat 5g, saturated fat 3g, fibre none, sugar 6g, salt 0.08g

A more grown-up flapjack, this one. The tangy plums and slightly bitter walnuts balance the sweet, oaty layers perfectly.

Sticky plum flapjack bars

450g/1lb fresh plums, halved, stoned and roughly sliced
½ tsp ground mixed spice
300g/10oz light muscovado sugar
350g/12oz butter, plus extra for greasing
300g/10oz oats (not jumbo)
140g/5oz plain flour
50g/2oz chopped walnut pieces
3 tbsp golden syrup

Takes 1 hour 20 minutes, plus cooling
Makes 18

1 Preheat the oven to 200°C/180°C fan/gas 6. Tip the plums into a bowl. Toss with the spice, 50g/2oz of the sugar and a small pinch of salt, then set aside to macerate.

2 Gently melt the butter in a pan. In a large bowl, mix the oats, flour, walnut pieces and remaining sugar, then stir in the butter and golden syrup to a loose flapjack mixture.

3 Grease a 20cm-square baking tin. Press half the oaty mix over the base, then spread the plums over in an even layer. Press the remaining oats over the plums so they are completely covered right to the sides of the tin. Bake for 45–50 minutes until dark golden and starting to crisp a little. Leave to cool completely, then cut into eighteen little bars. Will keep in an airtight container for 2 days or can be frozen for up to a month.

• Per bar 335 kcalories, protein 3g, carbohydrate 38g, fat 20g, saturated fat 11g, fibre 2g, sugar 22g, salt 0.34g

Use fresh or frozen berries for this unforgettably good treat.

Blackberry and coconut squares

250g/9oz self-raising flour
25g/1oz oats
280g/10oz brown soft sugar
200g/8oz cold butter, cut into pieces
75g/2½ oz desiccated coconut
2 medium eggs, beaten
350g/12oz frozen or fresh blackberries

Takes 1 hour, plus chilling and cooling
Makes 12

1 Preheat the oven to 180°C/160°C fan/ gas 4. Tip the flour, oats and sugar into a large bowl. Rub the butter into the flour mixture using your fingertips until only small pea-sized pieces remain. Stir through the coconut, then fill a teacup with the mixture and set this aside.
2 Stir the eggs into the remaining mixture in the bowl, then spread over the bottom of a lined baking tin, either 31x17cm or 21cm square. Smooth the surface with the back of a spoon, then scatter over the blackberries
3 Scatter over the reserved teacup of mixture and bake for 1 hour–1¼ hours until golden and cooked through (if you poke a skewer in, it should come out with moist crumbs but no wet mixture). Leave to cool, then remove from the tin and cut into squares.

• Per square 347 kcalories, protein 4g, carbohydrate 43g, fat 19g, saturated fat 12g, fibre 3g, sugar 26g, salt 0.5g

If you like rocky road, you'll really enjoy these. This recipe is endlessly versatile – use any other sweets instead of Turkish Delight, and try digestive or ginger biscuits, if you prefer.

Chocolate crunch bars

100g/4oz butter, roughly chopped
300g/10oz dark chocolate,
broken into squares
3 tbsp golden syrup
140g/5oz rich tea biscuits,
roughly crushed
12 pink marshmallows, quartered
(use scissors)
2 × 55g bars Turkish Delight,
halved and sliced

Takes 20 minutes, plus chilling
Makes 12

1 Gently melt the butter, chocolate and syrup in a pan over a low heat, stirring frequently until smooth, then cool for about 10 minutes. Line a 17cm-square baking tin with parchment.
2 Stir the biscuits and sweets into the pan until well mixed, then pour into the tin and spread the mixture roughly to level it. Chill until hard, then cut into fingers.

• Per bar 294 kcalories, protein 2g, carbohydrate 39g, fat 15g, saturated fat 9g, fibre 1g, sugar 31g, salt 0.29g

Melt-in-the-mouth shortbread fingers are so simple to make – and contain just four ingredients.

Shortbread

300g/10oz butter, softened
140g/5oz golden caster sugar,
plus extra 4 tbsp
300g/10oz plain flour
140g/5oz rice flour

Takes 35–40 minutes, plus chilling
and cooling • Makes 24

1 Put the butter and 140g/5oz sugar in a food processor, and whiz until smooth. Tip in both the flours and a pinch of salt, then pulse until the mixture comes together.
2 Using your hands, roughly spread out the mixture in a 20x30x4cm baking tin. Cover with cling film and smooth over until there are no wrinkles. Chill for at least 30 minutes and up to 2 days.
3 Preheat the oven to 180°C/160°C fan/ gas 4. Remove the cling film, then lightly score the shortbread all over with a fork. Sprinkle with the extra sugar, then bake for 20–25 minutes. Leave to cool in the tin, then cut into 24 thin slices. Shortbread will keep in an airtight container for up to 1 week.

• Per biscuit 188 kcalories, protein 2g, carbohydrate 23g, fat 11g, saturated fat 7g, fibre none, sugar 9g, salt 0.2g

This delicious bake has the most wonderful texture. It will keep in the fridge for up to 3 days – leave it on the tin base and cut off slices as you go.

Raspberry and white chocolate slice

375g pack ready-rolled shortcrust pastry
2 × 250g tubs mascarpone
100g/4oz golden caster sugar
100g/4oz ground almonds
2 large eggs
250g/9oz fresh raspberries
100g/4oz white chocolate, roughly chopped

Takes 40 minutes, plus cooling
Makes 16

1 Preheat the oven to 160°C/140°C fan/gas 3. Roll out the pastry a little more on a floured work surface and use to line either a 30x20cm tin or a Swiss roll tin. Line with greaseproof paper, fill with baking beans and cook for 10 minutes. Take out the beans and paper, then return to the oven for a further 5 minutes.
2 Whisk together the mascarpone, sugar, almonds and eggs until well blended. Fold in the raspberries and chocolate, then pour into the tin. Bake for 20–25 minutes until just set and lightly golden. Turn off the oven, open the door and leave the slice to cool gradually. For the best results, chill for at least 1 hour before slicing.

• Per slice 314 kcalories, protein 5g, carbohydrate 19g, fat 25g, saturated fat 12g, fibre 2g, sugar 13g, salt 0.18g

You'll probably have most of the ingredients for these bars in the cupboard already. For the best flavour and texture, choose an unsweetened muesli that's not too fruit filled.

Muesli fruit and nut bars

100g/4oz butter, plus extra
for greasing
100g/4oz light muscovado sugar
4 tbsp golden syrup
100g pack pecan nuts
350g/12oz unsweetened muesli
1 medium ripe banana, mashed

Takes 35 minutes, plus cooling
Makes 12

1 Preheat the oven to 180°C/160°C fan/gas 4. Butter and line the base of an 18x28cm (or 22cm-square) baking tin with baking parchment. Melt the butter, sugar and syrup in a medium pan on a low heat. Stir until the butter has melted and the sugar has dissolved. Cool slightly.

2 Chop half the nuts. Tip the muesli, banana and chopped nuts into the pan, and stir until well covered. Spoon into the prepared tin and press down with the back of the spoon until firmly packed.

3 Scatter with the whole nuts and press lightly into the mixture. Bake for 20–25 minutes until the muesli turns dark golden and the edges have started to crisp. Leave in the tin until cold, then loosen the edges with a knife. Cut into twelve slices. Keep in an airtight container for up to 5 days.

• Per bar 330 kcalories, protein 5g, carbohydrate 34g, fat 20g, saturated fat 5g, fibre 3g, added sugar 12g, salt 0.24g

These will be a big hit with children – they're sticky,
crunchy and chewy in one bite.

Squeamish squares

140g/5oz dark chocolate, broken into pieces (70% cocoa solids is good)
100g/4oz unsalted butter
4 tbsp golden syrup
100g/4oz Rice Krispies
50g/2oz dried blueberries
50g/2oz dried cranberries
100g/4oz mini marshmallows
50g/2oz white chocolate, broken into pieces
jelly snakes and bugs, to decorate

Takes 20 minutes, plus chilling • Makes 16 squares or 32 bite-sized chunks

1 Line a 20cm-square tin with baking parchment. Melt the dark chocolate, butter and golden syrup together in a pan over a low heat.

2 Put the Rice Krispies in a large bowl and mix in the blueberries, cranberries and marshmallows. Stir in the melted dark chocolate to coat. Spoon the mixture into the tin and spread out evenly. Chill in the fridge for at least 1 hour until set.

3 Remove from the tin and peel away the paper. Using a sharp knife, cut into sixteen squares or thirty-two bite-sized pieces. Melt the white chocolate in a small bowl set over a pan of barely simmering water, or in the microwave on High for 1 minute, stirring halfway through. Using a teaspoon, drizzle the white chocolate over the squares. Scatter with the jelly sweets, then leave to set before serving. Keep in an airtight container for up to 2 days.

• Per square 197 kcalories, protein 2g, carbohydrate 26g, fat 10g, saturated fat 6g, fibre 1g, sugar 17g, salt 0.15g

A dark-chocolate topping and melt-in-the-mouth almond shortbread
give this classic bake a very special twist.

Choc and nut caramel slice

140g/5oz unsalted butter, cold and
cut into cubes, plus extra
for greasing
175g/6oz plain flour
25g/1oz cornflour
50g/2oz golden caster sugar
85g/3oz blanched almonds, toasted
then finely chopped
seeds from 1 vanilla pod

FOR THE CARAMEL
200g/8oz golden caster sugar
142ml pot single cream
50g/2oz butter, cubed

FOR THE TOPPING
200g bar dark chocolate
(70% cocoa solids)
85g/3oz butter

Takes 1 hour 20 minutes, plus chilling
and cooling • Makes 16

1 Preheat the oven to 160°C/140°C fan/
gas 3. Lightly butter a shallow 20x23cm
baking tin. In a large bowl, sift the flours
together, stir in the sugar, almonds and a
pinch of salt. Rub in the butter and vanilla
seeds to make fine crumbs, then press firmly
into the tin. Freeze for 5 minutes, then bake
for 35–40 minutes. Cool.
2 For the caramel, put the sugar and
100ml/3½fl oz of water in a heavy-based
pan, heat gently until the sugar dissolves,
then turn up the heat until it turns a very dark
amber. Stir in the cream in four additions until
smooth – take care as it will bubble up. Stir in
the butter and ½ teaspoon of salt. Pour over
the shortbread and cool.
3 For the topping, melt the chocolate and
butter together then pour over the caramel
and smooth with the back of a spoon. Chill
for at least 30 minutes before cutting.

• Per slice 361 kcalories, protein 4g, carbohydrate 34g,
fat 24g, saturated fat 13g, fibre 2g, sugar 22g, salt 0.15g

Big American-style granola bars are top of the list in coffee-to-go shops. Packed with oats, seeds, fruits and nuts, they are the perfect snack food.

Granola bars

175g/6oz unsalted butter
140g/5oz clear honey
250g/9oz demerara sugar
350g/12oz porridge oats
1½ tsp ground cinnamon
85g/3oz pecan nuts or walnuts
85g/3oz raisins
85g/3oz dried papaya or mango, chopped
85g/3oz dried apricots, chopped
85g/3oz pumpkin seeds
50g/2oz ground almonds
50g/2oz sesame seeds

Takes 35 minutes, plus cooling
Makes 9

1 Preheat the oven to 190°C/170°C fan/ gas 5. Line the base of a 23cm-square cake tin with baking parchment. Melt the butter and honey in a pan, then stir in the sugar.
2 Cook over a low heat for 5 minutes, stirring until the sugar has dissolved. Bring to the boil, then boil for 12 minutes, stirring, until thickened into a smooth caramel sauce.
3 Mix together all the remaining ingredients and stir into the sauce until well combined. Spoon into the tin and press down well with the back of a warm, wet spoon. Bake for 15 minutes until just beginning to brown around the edges. Allow to cool.
4 Run a sharp knife around the sides of the tin to loosen. Turn out, then peel off the lining paper. Cool completely and cut into nine squares.

• Per bar 696 kcalories, protein 11g, carbohydrate 85g, fat 37g, saturated fat 12g, fibre 6g, added sugar 41g, salt 0.06g

These luscious bites are great for coffee lovers, and this all-in-one pan method means they're simple to make.

Moccachino slices

100g/4oz butter, plus extra for greasing
225g/8½oz dark brown soft sugar
2 large eggs
3 tbsp espresso coffee (or 3 tbsp boiling water with 1 tbsp instant coffee)
2 tsp baking powder
125g/4½oz plain flour

FOR THE TOPPING
284ml pot soured cream
300g/10oz white chocolate, broken into chunks
4 tsp caster sugar
cocoa powder, to dust

Takes 45 minutes, plus cooling
Makes 12

1 Preheat the oven to 180°C/160°C fan/gas 4 and butter and line the base and sides of a baking tin, about 30x23cm, with baking parchment.

2 Melt the butter in a large pan, stir in the sugar and mix well. Take off the heat and stir in the eggs and coffee. Tip in the baking powder and flour, then mix well. Pour into the baking sheet and bake for 20 minutes. Cool, then turn out on to a board.

3 Meanwhile, melt together the soured cream, white chocolate and sugar in a small bowl set over a pan of simmering water. Stir well, then leave to cool for 15 minutes. Spread all over the top of the cake. Shake over the cocoa powder to dust lightly, then leave to set. Cut into twelve squares and serve with a hot drink.

• Per slice 372 kcalories, protein 5g, carbohydrate 45g, fat 20g, saturated fat 12g, fibre 1g, sugar 36g, salt 0.51g

A no-bake treat. If you use chocolate with 70% cocoa solids you can even cut the mix into tasty slivers to serve with coffee.

Chocolate and ginger nut slices

100g/4oz unsalted butter, plus extra for greasing
185g/6½oz dark chocolate
2 tbsp golden syrup
225g/8½oz ginger biscuits, crushed
100g/4oz hazelnuts, toasted and chopped

Takes 25 minutes, plus chilling
Makes 8

1 Lightly butter an 18cm-round sandwich tin. Put the butter, 100g/4oz of the chocolate and the syrup into a heatproof bowl, and set over a pan of simmering water. Stir occasionally, until melted.

2 Remove from the heat and stir in the crushed biscuit and three-quarters of the nuts. Press the mixture into the tin. Melt the remaining chocolate, then spoon on top and sprinkle over the remaining nuts. Chill for at least 1 hour. Cut into wedges to serve.

• Per slice 433 kcalories, protein 4g, carbohydrate 39g, fat 30g, saturated fat 13g, fibre 2g, added sugar 20g, salt 0.68g

The original schooldays classic is still hard to beat!

Classic flapjacks

175g/6oz butter
100g/4oz light muscovado sugar
1 generous tbsp golden syrup
225g/8½oz porridge oats

Takes 40–45 minutes, plus cooling
Makes 10

1 Preheat the oven to 170°C/150°C fan/ gas 3. Grease and line a 20cm-square baking tin with baking parchment. Put the butter, sugar and syrup into a heavy-based pan over a low heat, and stir until everything has melted together into a dark syrup.
2 Off the heat, tip in the oats and stir to coat. Tip and spread the mixture into the tin. Bake for 20–25 minutes – the mixture should be golden brown with slightly more colour around the edges. Take it out of the oven and, while it's still hot, mark out ten bars on the surface. Then, when just warm, cut along the markings. Once completely cold, loosen the edges with a round-bladed knife. Tip out on to a plate or board, peel off the parchment and break into pieces. The flapjacks will keep in a biscuit tin for up to 3 days.

• Per flapjack 259 kcalories, protein 4g, carbohydrate 27g, fat 16g, saturated fat 9g, fibre 2g, added sugar 12g, salt 0.3g

An Australian speciality, Lamingtons will delight the tastebuds with their combination of chocolate, vanilla cream and coconut.

Lamingtons

oil, for greasing
6 large eggs
140g/5oz golden caster sugar
200g/8oz self-raising flour
25g/1oz butter, melted

FOR THE VANILLA CREAM
250g/9oz icing sugar, sifted
1 tsp vanilla extract
50g/2oz butter, softened
2 tsp milk

FOR THE ICING
300g/10oz icing sugar
4 tbsp cocoa powder
25g/1oz butter
125ml/4fl oz milk
140g/5oz desiccated coconut

Takes 1½ hours, plus cooling and setting
Makes 16

1 Preheat the oven to 180°C/160°C fan/ gas 4. Grease a 23cm-square cake tin. Beat the eggs and sugar until pale and thick. Fold in the flour, butter and 5 tablespoons of hot water. Pour into the tin and bake for 35 minutes until firm. Turn out on to a wire rack and cool.

2 Whip the vanilla-cream ingredients together until very thick and creamy. Cut the cake into 16, then slice each square horizontally in half and sandwich together with the cream.

3 Sift the sugar and cocoa for the icing into a bowl. Microwave the butter and milk on High for 1 minute (or in a pan on a low heat) until the butter has melted. Stir into the sugar mixture, spoon over each square and lift with a fork so the icing drains off. Put on a wire rack and sprinkle with the coconut. Leave to set.

• Per square 360 kcalories, protein 4.8g, carbohydrate 57g, fat 14g, saturated fat 9g, fibre 2g, sugar 46g, salt 0.33g

Polenta (sometimes called fine cornmeal) gives these cakes their yellow colour and soft texture. If you'd rather, use a total of 200g/8oz self-raising flour instead.

Swirly lemon drizzle fingers

200g/8oz butter, well softened, plus extra for greasing
200g/8oz golden caster sugar
4 large eggs
100g/4oz fine polenta or fine cornmeal
140g/5oz self-raising flour
zest of 3 lemons

FOR THE SWIRL AND DRIZZLE
4 tbsp lemon curd
5 tbsp golden or white caster sugar
zest and juice of 1 lemon

Takes 55 minutes, plus cooling
Makes 18

1 Preheat the oven to 180°C/160°C fan/gas 4. Butter then line a rectangular baking tin or small roasting tin, about 20x30cm, with baking parchment.
2 Put the cake ingredients and a pinch of salt into a large bowl, then beat until creamy and smooth. Scoop into the tin, then level the top. Spoon the lemon curd over the batter in thick stripes then swirl into the cake – not too much or you won't see them once cooked. Bake for 35 minutes or until golden and risen. Don't open the oven before 30 minutes' cooking is up. Leave the cake in the tin for 10 minutes or until just cool enough to handle. Carefully transfer to a wire cooling rack.
3 For the drizzle, mix 4 tablespoons of the sugar with the lemon juice and spoon it over the warm cake. Toss the lemon zest with the remaining sugar and sprinkle over the top. Cut into fingers when cool.

• Per finger 214 kcalories, protein 3g, carbohydrate 27g, fat 11g, saturated fat 6g, fibre none, sugar 17g, salt 0.3g

A wonderfully moist cake that is reminiscent of old-fashioned gingerbread. Serve it for tea or heat up a thick slice in the microwave and have it for pud with a dollop of custard.

Rhubarb spice cake

140g/5oz butter, softened, plus extra for greasing
300g/10oz self-raising flour
2 tsp ground mixed spice
1 tsp ground ginger
100g/4oz dark muscovado sugar
250g/9oz golden syrup
1 tsp bicarbonate of soda
2 large eggs, beaten
300g/10oz rhubarb, cut into short lengths
icing sugar, for dusting

Takes 1 hour 10 minutes, plus cooling
Makes 12

1 Preheat the oven to 180°C/160°C fan/ gas 4 and put the kettle on. Butter and line a deep 20cm-square cake tin. Sift the flour and spices into a bowl. Beat together the butter and sugar until light and fluffy in a food processor, then beat in the golden syrup. Dissolve the bicarbonate of soda in 200ml/ 7fl oz boiling water, then gradually pour through the spout of the processor. Pulse in the flour mix, then add the eggs, mixing briefly. Remove the bowl from the processor, then gently stir in the rhubarb.
2 Pour the mixture into the tin and bake for 50 minutes–1 hour, until the cake feels firm to the touch and springs back when pressed. Cool in the tin for 5 minutes, then turn out and cool on a wire rack. Lightly dust with icing sugar.

• Per slice 290 kcalories, protein 4g, carbohydrate 46g, fat 11g, saturated fat 7g, fibre 1g, sugar 27g, salt 0.89g

A square of classic carrot cake contains 315 kcalories and 20g fat (5g saturated fat). This one contains 217 kcalories and 9g fat (1g saturated fat) – so now you really can have your cake and eat it!

Better-for-you carrot cake

zest and juice of 1 medium orange
140g/5oz raisins
125ml/4fl oz rapeseed oil,
plus extra for greasing
115g/4oz self-raising flour
115g/4oz plain wholemeal flour
1 tsp baking powder, plus a pinch
1 tsp bicarbonate of soda
1 rounded tsp ground cinnamon
2 large eggs
140g/5oz dark muscovado sugar
280g/10oz finely grated carrot

FOR THE FROSTING
100g/4oz light soft cheese, straight
from the fridge
100g/4oz Quark
3 tbsp icing sugar, sifted
½ tsp finely grated orange zest
1 tsp fresh lemon juice

Takes 1½ hours, plus cooling
Makes 16

1 Preheat the oven to 160°C/140°C fan/ gas 3. Mix the orange zest and 3 tablespoons of juice with the raisins. Oil then line the base of a deep 20cm-square cake tin. Mix the flours, 1 teaspoon of baking powder, the bicarbonate of soda and cinnamon.
2 Separate one egg. Add the remaining whole egg to the yolk, then whisk in the sugar for 1–2 minutes until thick. Whisk in the oil. Fold in the flour mix in two goes. Whisk the egg white and pinch of bicarbonate of soda to soft peaks.
3 Fold the carrot, raisins and juice into the flour mixture. Fold in the whisked white, then pour into the tin. Bake for 1 hour until risen and firm or until a skewer inserted in the centre comes out clean. Cool for 5 minutes in the tin, then on a wire rack.
4 For the frosting, beat everything together until smooth. Swirl over the cake before slicing.

• Per square 217 kcalories, protein 4g, carbohydrate 31g, fat 9g, saturated fat 1g, fibre 2g, sugar 21g, salt 0.52g

There's no need to buy chocolate with a high cocoa content for this recipe – once melted with dark muscovado you'll have all the fudgy, chocolatey flavour you could ever need.

Chocolate and orange fudge squares

175g/6oz butter, plus
extra for greasing
200g/8oz dark chocolate,
broken into cubes
200g/8oz dark muscovado sugar
3 large eggs, separated
140g/5oz plain flour
1 tsp vanilla extract
zest of 1 orange

FOR THE TOPPING
200g tub soft cheese
½ tsp vanilla extract
50g/2oz icing sugar

Takes 40 minutes, plus cooling
Makes 15

1 Preheat the oven to 180°C/160°C fan/ gas 4. Butter and line a traybake tin, about 23x23cm. Put the chocolate, sugar and butter in a pan, then heat very gently for about 5 minutes, stirring every minute until the butter and chocolate have melted. Leave to cool for 10 minutes. Beat in the egg yolks, flour, vanilla and half the orange zest.

2 Put the egg whites into a very clean large bowl, then whisk until they stand up in peaks. Stir a spoonful of the whites into the chocolate mix to loosen it, then carefully fold in the rest with a metal spoon. Pour the mix into the tin, then bake for 25 minutes or until evenly risen and just firm to the touch. Cool in the tin, then cut into squares.

3 Beat together the cheese, vanilla, sugar and remaining orange zest until smooth. Spread over each chocolate square and serve.

• Per square 289 kcalories, protein 5g, carbohydrate 34g, fat 16g, saturated fat 9g, fibre 1g, sugar 27g, salt 0.37g

With juicy peach and raspberry in every bite, these squares are special enough for summer afternoon tea, or served warm as dessert with a scoop of ice cream.

Peach melba squares

250g pack unsalted butter, plus extra for greasing
300g/10oz golden caster sugar
1 tsp vanilla extract
3 large eggs
200g/8oz self-raising flour
50g/2oz ground almonds
2 just ripe peaches, stoned, halved, then each half cut into 3
100g/4oz raspberries
a handful of flaked almonds
1 tbsp icing sugar, to dust

Takes 1 hour 20 minutes, plus cooling
Makes 12

1 Butter and line a traybake or small roasting tin, about 20x30cm. Preheat the oven to 180°C/160°C fan/gas 4. Gently melt the butter in a large pan, cool for 5 minutes, add the sugar, vanilla and eggs, then beat until smooth with a wooden spoon. Stir in the flour, almonds and ¼ teaspoon of salt.
2 Tip the mix into the tin, then lay the peach slices evenly on top – that way each square of cake will have a bite of fruit. Scatter the raspberries and almonds over, then bake for 1 hour–1 hour 10 minutes, covering with foil after 40 minutes. Test with a skewer; the middle should have just a tiny hint of squidginess, which will firm up once the cake cools. Cool in the tin for 20 minutes, then lift out on to a wire cooling rack. Once cold, dredge with icing sugar, then cut into squares.

• Per square 385 kcalories, protein 5g, carbohydrate 43g, fat 23g, saturated fat 12g, fibre 2g, sugar 31g, salt 0.22g

For an even more delicious treat, pop these tiny temptations
into a low oven to warm through quickly before serving.

Chocolate brownie chunks
with chocolate dip

200g/8oz dark chocolate,
broken into chunks
100g/4oz milk chocolate,
broken into chunks
85g/3oz butter
100g/4oz light muscovado sugar
85g/3oz dark muscovado sugar
3 large eggs, at room temperature
and lightly beaten
140g/5oz plain flour
140g/5oz walnuts, roughly chopped
200g/8oz natural yogurt

Takes 45 minutes, plus cooling
Serves 8

1 Preheat the oven to 180°C/160°C fan/
gas 4 and line the base of a shallow
20cm-square baking tin with baking
parchment. Melt 100g of the dark chocolate,
all of the milk chocolate and the butter in
a heatproof bowl over a pan of simmering
water. Stir in the sugars off the heat. Cool
for a little while you prepare the rest of
the ingredients.
2 Stir the eggs into the chocolate mixture,
followed by the flour, walnuts and a pinch
of salt until really well combined. Pour the
mixture into the prepared tin, then bake
for 25–30 minutes until an inserted skewer
comes out with sticky crumbs. Cool in the tin.
3 For the dip, gently melt the remaining dark
chocolate as above, then stir into the yogurt
and chill. To serve, cut the brownies into
chunks, then spoon the dip into small bowls.

• Per chunk 588 kcalories, protein 11g, carbohydrate 63g,
fat 35g, saturated fat 14g, fibre 2g, sugar 49g, salt 0.34g

Make the most of the short gooseberry season with these scrumptious squares. If you're too late, though, frozen berries work well too.

Gooseberry and almond streusel squares

250g/9oz chilled butter, chopped
250g/9oz self-raising flour
125g/4oz ground almonds
125g/4oz light muscovado sugar
350g/12oz gooseberries,
fresh or frozen
85g/3oz caster sugar,
plus extra to sprinkle
50g/2oz flaked almonds

Takes 1 hour 5 minutes–1¼ hours,
plus cooling • Makes about 8

1 Preheat the oven to 190°C/170°C fan/ gas 5. Line a 27x18cm baking tin with baking parchment. Rub the butter into the flour, almonds and sugar to make crumbs, then firmly press two-thirds of the mixture on to the base and sides of the tin. Toss the gooseberries with the caster sugar, then scatter over the top.

2 Mix the flaked almonds into the remaining crumbs, then scatter over the gooseberries. Bake for 50 minutes–1 hour until golden and the fruit is bubbling a little around the edges. Dredge with more caster sugar, then cool in the tin. Serve cut into about eight squares.

• Per square 589 kcalories, protein 8g, carbohydrate 56g, fat 38g, saturated fat 17g, fibre 4g, sugar 32g, salt 0.78g

Do you wish you could find a nasty-free cake for the kids' party? If so, this is the recipe for you. Add colour with candles and flags rather than the usual bright sweeties and icing.

Chocolate birthday cake

140g/5oz butter, plus extra
for greasing
175g/6oz golden caster sugar
2 large eggs
225g/8½oz self-raising
wholemeal flour
50g/2oz cocoa powder
½ tsp bicarbonate of soda
250g/9oz natural yogurt

TO DECORATE
300g/10oz golden icing sugar
2 tbsp cocoa powder
1 tbsp butter, melted
3–4 tbsp boiling water
50g/2oz each milk, dark and white
chocolate, broken into squares
and melted separately

Takes 40 minutes, plus cooling
Makes 12

1 Preheat the oven to 180°C/160°C fan/gas 4. Butter and line the base of an 18x28cm cakebake or tray tin. Beat the butter and sugar together until creamy, then add the eggs gradually until fluffy.
2 Sieve the flour, cocoa and bicarbonate of soda into the bowl, then tip in any bran left in the sieve. Stir in the yogurt to a smooth mixture then spoon into the tin. Bake for 20–25 minutes until risen and springy. Cool for 5 minutes, then turn out on to a wire rack.
3 Sieve the icing sugar and cocoa into a bowl, and add the butter and 2 tablespoons of the hot water. Stir together until smooth. Spread over the cold cake using a palette knife dipped in the remaining hot water.
4 Spoon the melted chocolates into separate freezer bags. Snip the ends off then pipe shapes on top of the cake. Once set, cut into squares and push in some candles.

• Per slice 432 kcalories, protein 6g, carbohydrate 65g, fat 18g, saturated fat 10g, fibre 3g, sugar 51g, salt 0.41g

If you're looking for a slice with spice, try this deliciously moist ginger cake. If you can resist cutting it, the cake is best eaten a day or two after baking, when it gets even stickier.

Triple ginger and spice cake

250g pack butter
250g/9oz dark muscovado sugar
250g/9oz black treacle
300ml/10fl oz milk
2 large eggs
100g/4oz stem ginger in syrup, finely chopped
375g/13oz plain flour
2 tsp bicarbonate of soda
1 tsp ground allspice
2 tsp ground ginger

FOR THE ICING
3 tbsp ginger syrup from the jar
5 tbsp icing sugar, sifted

Takes 1 hour 20 minutes, plus cooling
Makes 16

1 Butter and line a 23cm-square baking tin (or use a shallow roasting tin, about 30x20cm). Preheat the oven to 160°C/140°C fan/gas 3. Gently melt together the butter, sugar and treacle in a pan. Take off the heat then stir in the milk. Beat in the eggs.
2 Mix the chopped ginger and dry ingredients in a large bowl, and make a well in the centre. Pour in the melted mix then stir to a smooth batter. Pour into the tin, then bake for 1 hour until risen and firm and a skewer inserted into the centre comes out clean. Resist taking a peek beforehand as this cake can easily sink. Cool in the tin, then ice (or wrap well and keep in a cool, dry place for up to a week).
3 Stir together the syrup and icing sugar to make the icing and drizzle over. Cut into sixteen squares.

• Per square 360 kcalories, protein 4g carbohydrate 57g, fat 14g, saturated fat 9g, fibre none, sugar 39g, salt 0.81g

Everyone will love this tasty bake with its Bakewell-like
filling and layer of tangy cherry jam.

Classic cherry and almond slice

375g pack ready-rolled shortcrust
pastry
100g/4oz butter, softened
100g/4oz golden caster sugar
1 large egg, beaten
25g/1oz ground rice
50g/2oz ground almonds
50g/2oz desiccated coconut
50g/2oz walnuts, roughly chopped
5 tbsp cherry jam
100g/4oz undyed glacé cherries

Takes 1 hour, plus cooling • Makes 16

1 Preheat the oven to 180°C/160°C fan/
gas 4 and line the base of an 18x27cm (or
thereabouts) baking tin with greaseproof
paper. Line the base and sides with the
pastry, trim the edges, then chill while you
make the filling.
2 Beat the butter and sugar together until
fluffy, then gradually add the egg until creamy.
Stir in the ground rice, almonds, coconut and
nuts. Spread the jam over the pastry, then
dollop the almond mix on top. Don't worry
if there are some little gaps as the filling will
spread during baking.
3 Dot the cherries over the top, then bake
for 40–45 minutes until light golden and
set. Check after 30 minutes – if the top is
browning too quickly, cover loosely with
greaseproof paper. Cool in the tin; cut into
sixteen slices.

• Per slice 275 kcalories, protein 3g, carbohydrate 27g,
fat 18g, saturated fat 8g, fibre 1g, sugar 15g, salt 0.36g

If you're looking for a treat for afternoon tea, or something to make for a cake sale, try this crunchy-topped tray bake.

Coconut carrot slices

250g pack unsalted butter, plus extra for greasing
300g/10oz light muscovado sugar
1 tsp vanilla extract
3 large eggs
200g/8oz self-raising flour
50g/2oz desiccated coconut
200g/8oz carrot, grated
2 tsp ground mixed spice

FOR THE TOPPING
85g/3oz desiccated coconut
25g/1oz light muscovado sugar
25g/1oz melted butter

Takes 50 minutes, plus cooling
Makes about 15

1 Butter and line a traybake or small roasting tin, about 20x30cm. Preheat the oven to 180°C/160°C fan/gas 4. Gently melt the butter in a large pan, cool for 5 minutes, add the sugar, vanilla and eggs, then beat until smooth with a wooden spoon. Stir in the flour, coconut, carrot, spice and ¼ teaspoon of salt.
2 Tip the mix into the tin, then bake for 30 minutes. Meanwhile, evenly mix the coconut and sugar for the topping, then stir in the melted butter. Smooth this over the cake, then bake for 10 minutes more until golden and a skewer inserted into the centre comes out clean. Cool, then cut into about fifteen slices.

• Per slice 347 kcalories, protein 4g, carbohydrate 35g, fat 22g, saturated fat 15g, fibre 2g, sugar 25g, salt 0.22g

Deliciously chocolatey, yet beautifully light brownies. One classic brownie contains 314 kcalories and 19g fat, but these feel-good treats have only 191 kcalories and 11g fat.

Better-for-you chocolate brownies

oil, for greasing
85g/3oz plain flour
25g/1oz cocoa powder
½ tsp bicarbonate of soda
100g/4oz golden caster sugar
50g/2oz light muscovado sugar
85g/3oz dark chocolate, 70% cocoa
solids, melted then cooled
½ tsp coffee granules
1 tsp vanilla extract
2 tbsp buttermilk
1 large egg, beaten
100g/4oz mayonnaise

Takes 55 minutes, plus cooling
Makes 12

1 Preheat the oven to 180°C/160°C fan/ gas 4. Lightly oil and line the base of a 19cm-square cake tin. Combine the flour, cocoa and bicarbonate of soda. Stir both the sugars into the cooled chocolate with the coffee, vanilla and buttermilk. Stir in 1 tablespoon of warm water. Beat in the egg, then stir in the mayonnaise just until smooth and glossy. Sift over the flour and cocoa mix, then gently fold in with a spatula.
2 Spread the mix evenly into the tin. Bake for 30 minutes. When a skewer is inserted into the middle, it should come out with just a few moist crumbs sticking to it. Leave in the tin until completely cold, then loosen the sides with a round-bladed knife. Turn out on to a board, peel off the lining paper and cut into twelve squares.

• Per brownie 191 kcalories, protein 2g, carbohydrate 23g, fat 11g, saturated fat 3g, fibre 1g, sugar 16g, salt 0.28g

These little pastries are particularly good with a strong
cup of coffee at the end of a meal.

Walnut and rosewater baklava

FOR THE SYRUP
140g/5oz caster sugar
250ml/9fl oz hot water
2 tbsp rosewater

FOR THE LAYERS
100g/4oz butter, melted, plus extra
for greasing
200g/8oz walnuts, finely chopped
50g/2oz caster sugar
1 heaped tsp ground cinnamon
½ tsp ground cloves
400g pack filo pastry (you will
need 12 sheets)

Takes 35 minutes, plus cooling
Makes 16

1 For the syrup, dissolve the sugar in the
water in a pan over a low heat, then boil for
15 minutes, or until thickened but not coloured.
Stir in the rosewater and set aside to cool.
2 Meanwhile, lightly butter a 15x25cm baking
tray and mix the walnuts, sugar and spices
together. Unroll the pastry, peel off twelve
sheets and, keeping the layers together, cut a
rectangle just big enough to fit inside the tin.
Re-wrap any leftover pastry for another time.
3 Preheat the oven to 180°C/160°C fan/
gas 4. Brush four pastry sheets with the
melted butter and use them to cover the
bottom of the baking sheet. Top with half of
the nut mix then repeat, using four sheets of
buttered pastry for each layer and finishing
with a layer of pastry. Using a sharp knife, cut
diagonal lines all the way through to create
small diamonds. Bake for 15–20 minutes until
golden. Pour the syrup over, then cool.

• Per diamond 169 kcalories, protein 2g, carbohydrate 16g, fat
11g, saturated fat 3g, fibre 0.3g, added sugar 11g, salt 0.29g

The base of this cake is like a child-friendly brownie – not too rich, but lovely and moist. You can simply top with some chocolate spread and dark biscuits for gravestones, or go all out with this ghostly idea.

Haunted graveyard cake

85g/3oz cocoa powder
200g/8oz self-raising flour
375g/13oz light muscovado sugar
4 large eggs
200ml/7fl oz milk
175ml/6fl oz vegetable oil

TO DECORATE
1 egg white
50g/2oz icing sugar
200ml/7fl oz single cream
200g/8oz dark chocolate,
finely chopped
7 rich tea finger biscuits
100g/4oz double chocolate cookies,
whizzed to crumbs
25g/1oz white chocolate, melted
and cooled for 10 minutes
edible silver balls, to decorate

Takes 2¾ hours, plus cooling
Serves 12

1 Preheat the oven to 110°C/90°C fan/gas ¼. Line a baking sheet with parchment. Whip the egg white until stiff. Gradually whisk in the sugar until stiff and shiny. Spoon into a food bag, cut a 1.5cm hole in one corner then squeeze out fifteen ghosts. Bake for 1 hour until crisp.
2 Grease and line a traybake tin (about 20x30x5cm). Turn up the oven to 180°C/160°C fan/gas 4. For the cake, sift the dry ingredients into a bowl. Beat the wet ingredients together, then stir into the dry until smooth. Pour the cake mix into the tin; bake for 30 minutes then cool.
3 Bring the cream to the boil then stir in the chocolate off the heat. Once smooth, paint thinly over the biscuits. Smooth the rest over the cake. Sprinkle with cookie crumbs.
4 Use white chocolate to stick two silver eyes on to ghosts and pipe on to gravestones. Once set, add the decorations.

• Per slice 601 kcalories, protein 7.5g, carbohydrate 79g, fat 30g, saturated fat 9g, fibre 2.5g, sugar 55g, salt 0.52g

A simple crowd-pleasing cake that will keep well. The fudgy topping is a great recipe to have up your sleeve for children's birthday cakes, too.

Sticky chocolate-drop cakes

250g pack unsalted butter,
plus extra to grease
300g/10oz golden caster sugar
1 tsp vanilla extract
3 large eggs
200g/8oz self-raising flour
50g/2oz cocoa powder
100g/4oz milk chocolate drops

FOR THE TOPPING
85g/3oz butter
85g/3oz golden caster sugar
200g/8oz light condensed milk
50g/2oz milk chocolate drops,
plus extra to decorate

Takes 45 minutes, plus cooling •
Makes 15

1 Butter and line a traybake or small roasting tin, about 20x30cm. Preheat the oven to 180°C/160°C fan/gas 4. Gently melt the butter in a large pan, cool for 5 minutes, then add the sugar, vanilla and eggs, then beat until smooth with a wooden spoon. Stir in the flour, cocoa and ¼ teaspoon of salt. Stir in the chocolate drops then bake for 35 minutes until risen all over and an inserted skewer comes out with a few damp crumbs.
2 For the topping, gently heat the butter and sugar together until both are melted. Stir in the condensed milk and bring to the boil. Cool for 5 minutes, then stir in the chocolate drops to melt. Spread over the cold cake, scatter with more chocolate drops and cut into fifteen squares.

• Per square 433 kcalories, protein 5g, carbohydrate 54g, fat 24g, saturated fat 14g, fibre 1g, sugar 42g, salt 0.31g

Turn an old loaf into a nostalgic slice of the past. Bread pudding can be served hot with custard, but it is especially good cold and cut into squares for picnics and lunchboxes.

Bread pudding

500g/1lb 2oz white or wholemeal bread
500g/1lb 2oz mixed dried fruit
85g/3oz cut mixed peel
1 tbsp ground mixed spice
600ml/1 pint milk
2 large eggs, beaten
140g/5oz light muscovado sugar
zest of 1 lemon (optional)
100g/4oz butter, melted
2 tbsp demerara sugar

Takes 1 hour 40 minutes, plus soaking and cooling • Serves 9

1 Tear the bread into a large mixing bowl and add the dried fruit, peel and spice. Pour in the milk, then stir or scrunch the mixture through your fingers to mix everything well and completely break up the bread. Add the eggs, muscovado sugar and lemon zest, if using. Stir well, then set aside for 15 minutes to soak.

2 Preheat the oven to 180°C/160°C fan/gas 4. Butter and line the base of a non-stick 20cm-square cake tin (not one with a loose base). Stir the melted butter into the pudding mixture, tip into the tin, then scatter with demerara. Bake for 1½ hours until firm and golden, covering with foil if it starts to brown too much. Turn out of the tin and strip off the paper. Cut into nine large squares and serve warm.

• Per square 510 kcalories, protein 10g, carbohydrate 94g, fat 13g, saturated fat 7g, fibre 3g, sugar 67g, salt 1.15g

Shop-bought marzipan makes a clever almond base for fruit tarts. Replace strawberries with whatever's in season, if you like. Thinly sliced apples, plums or apricots would be particularly good.

Individual strawberry & almond tarts

375g pack ready-rolled puff pastry
25g/1oz butter, melted
200g/8oz marzipan, thinly sliced
400g/14oz large strawberries, hulled and sliced
25g/1oz golden caster sugar
25g/1oz toasted flaked almonds
vanilla ice cream, to serve

Takes 40 minutes • Makes 6

1 Preheat the oven to 220°C/200°C fan/ gas 7. Unravel the pastry and prick the surface with a fork. Cut into six squares and put on a non-stick baking sheet.
2 Lightly brush the edges of the squares with a little of the melted butter and put a couple of slices of marzipan on the top of each. Lay two rows of strawberry slices down the side of each tart and a third over the gap in the middle. Drizzle the tarts with the remaining melted butter and sprinkle with sugar. Bake for about 20–25 minutes, until golden brown on the base. Scatter the toasted almonds over the top and serve warm with a scoop of vanilla ice cream.

• Per serving 473 kcalories, protein 7g, carboyhdrate 49g, fat 29g, saturated fat 10g, fibre 3g, sugar 32g, salt 0.73g

These are flavoured with bourbon, the American-style whiskey from the Kentucky area of the US. If you don't have small tart tins, you can make a large pie in a 23cm-round tin and bake it for 40 minutes.

American pecan pies

300g/10oz plain flour
150g/5oz melted butter
50g/2oz golden caster sugar

FOR THE FILLING
175g/6oz pecan nut halves
4 large eggs
85g/3oz light muscovado sugar
175g/6oz golden syrup
1 tsp vanilla extract
2 tbsp bourbon
50g/2oz melted butter
a dollop of double cream or
crème fraîche, to serve

Takes 1 hour 10 minutes, plus chilling
Makes 6

1 Preheat the oven to 190°C/170°C fan/ gas 5. Work the flour, butter and sugar together with your hands until well mixed, then press on to the base and up the sides of six 10cm fluted tart tins. Put on to a baking sheet.

2 Reserve 36 pecan halves and roughly chop the rest. Beat together the eggs, sugar, syrup, vanilla, bourbon, melted butter and chopped pecans, and spoon into the tart cases. Top each one with six pecan halves, then bake for 20–25 minutes until golden and set. The filling will rise up as it bakes, but will settle back as it cools. Best served with a dollop of double cream or crème fraîche on the side.

• Per pie 871 kcalories, protein 13g, carbohydrate 89g, fat 53g, saturated fat 20g, fibre 3g, sugar 50g, salt 0.87g

The perfect sweet offering for the holiday period:
fruity and spicy but without any mincemeat.

Festive muffin tarts

450g/1lb plain flour, plus
extra for dusting
250g/9oz cold salted butter, cut
into small pieces
25g/1oz ground almonds
50g/2oz golden caster sugar
1 egg yolk, beaten

FOR THE FILLING
300g/10oz ground almonds
250g/9oz golden caster sugar
100g/4oz currants
100g/4oz sultanas
50g/2oz flaked almonds
2 tsp ground cinnamon
1 tsp ground nutmeg
1 tsp ground mixed spice
200g/8oz butter, melted
4 large eggs, beaten
finely grated zest and juice of
1 lemon and 1 orange
icing sugar, for dusting

Takes 1 hour 20 minutes • Makes 24

1 First, make the pastry. Measure 150ml/
¼ pint water in a jug. Rub together the flour
and butter until the mixture looks like crumbs.
Stir in the ground almonds and sugar then
add the yolk and a little of the water, stirring
with a knife. Gradually work in the rest of the
water, stirring until you have a soft pastry ball.
Chill for 30 minutes.
2 Preheat the oven to 200°C/180°C fan/
gas 6. For the filling, mix the dry ingredients
in a large bowl. Stir in the butter, eggs,
orange and lemon zests and juice.
3 Roll out the pastry on a lightly floured
surface to about 5mm thickness. Cut out
about 24 rounds with a 10cm-round cutter.
Line two 12-hole muffin tins, spoon in the
filling then bake for 20–25 minutes until pale
golden. Turn out on to a wire rack and dust
with icing sugar. Lovely served warm or cold.

• Per tart 394 kcalories, protein 7g, carbohydrate 36g,
fat 26g, saturated fat 11g, fibre 2g, added sugar none,
salt 0.41g

These are just as delicious as traditional mince pies, but a little lighter. Now there's no reason not to enjoy more than one!•

Orange, cranberry and almond mince pies

200g/8oz very cold butter, cubed
400g/14oz plain flour, plus extra for dusting
100g/4oz golden caster sugar
100g/4oz ground almonds
zest of 2 oranges
2 tbsp milk (or use fresh orange juice)
100g/4oz frozen cranberries
410g jar good-quality mincemeat
a handful of flaked almonds
2 tsp icing sugar, plus extra to dust
200ml pot crème fraîche, to serve

Takes 35 minutes, plus chilling
Makes 24

1 Put the butter and flour into a food processor, then whiz until the butter has disappeared. Pulse in the sugar, almonds and half the orange zest. Add the milk or orange juice and pulse to a rough dough. Tip on to the work surface, press together and shape into a smooth disk. Chill for 15 minutes.

2 Roll out the dough on a floured surface to the thickness of a £1 coin. Using an 8cm cutter, stamp out 24 circles, and use to line the wells of two 12-hole bun tins.

3 Preheat the oven to 200°C/180°C fan/gas 6. Mix the cranberries and mincemeat, then spoon into the cases. Scatter each pie with a few flaked almonds. Bake for 18–20 minutes until the pastry and almonds are golden. Stir the icing sugar and remaining zest into the crème fraîche. Dust the tarts with the extra icing sugar and serve with the crème fraîche.

• Per serving 213 kcalories, protein 3g, carbohydrate 29g, fat 10g, saturated fat 5g, fibre 2g, sugar 14g, salt 0.14g

Chelsea buns meet pecan pie in these sticky breakfast treats.

Cinnamon–pecan sticky buns

450g/1lb strong white flour
50g/2oz golden caster sugar
85g/3oz cold butter, cut
into small pieces
7g sachet dried yeast
2 large eggs, beaten
150ml/¼ pint full-fat milk
vegetable oil, for greasing

FOR THE FILLING
2 tsp ground cinnamon
85g/3oz light brown soft sugar
100g/4oz pecan nuts

FOR THE TOPPING
125g/4½oz melted butter, plus extra
125ml/4fl oz maple syrup
50g/2oz light brown soft sugar
100g/4oz pecan nuts,
roughly chopped

Takes 1 hour, plus rising and cooling
Makes 16

1 Mix the flour, sugar and 1 teaspoon of salt, then rub in the butter to fine crumbs. Tip in the yeast, eggs and milk then mix to a soft dough. Knead for 10 minutes until elastic then tip into an oiled bowl. Cover and leave to rise for 1 hour or until doubled in size. For the filling, whiz everything in a processor until fine.
2 Knead the dough and split it in two. Roll each piece to a 25x35cm rectangle. Brush with half the melted butter, then sprinkle the filling over. Roll up from the long edge, then pinch to seal. Slice both pieces into eight.
3 Grease two 20x30cm baking sheets. Mix the remaining topping ingredients and spread over the sheets. Sit the buns on top, spacing them well apart. Cover with lightly oiled cling film and leave for 30 minutes to rise.
4 Meanwhile, preheat the oven to 180°C/ 160°C fan/gas 4. Bake for 30 minutes until golden and firm. Serve warm, sticky-side up.

• Per bun 731 kcalories, protein 12g, carbohydrate 80g, fat 43g, saturated fat 16g, fibre 3g, sugar 36g, salt 1.13g

These dainty tarts would be wonderful for tea, or as a special dessert.

Little blueberry cream tarts

100g/4oz butter, softened
100g/4oz golden caster sugar
100g/4oz blanched hazelnuts,
finely ground in a
food processor
250g tub mascarpone
2–3 tbsp milk
3 tbsp good-quality lemon curd

FOR THE TOPPING
25g/1oz golden caster sugar
2 × 125g punnets blueberries

Takes 35–45 minutes • Makes 24

1 Preheat the oven to 180°C/160°C fan/ gas 4. Beat the butter and sugar together with a wooden spoon until soft and creamy. Mix in the hazelnuts.

2 Put a heaped teaspoon of the mixture into the wells of two 12-hole non-stick muffin tins. Bake for 10 minutes until golden and slightly risen. Cool for 5 minutes until firm, then ease each tart from the tins with a small knife.

3 For the topping, gently dissolve the sugar in 1 tablespoon of water in a pan set over a medium heat, then bring to the boil for 30 seconds only. Off the heat, tip in the blueberries. Stir, then cool.

4 Beat the mascarpone with the milk to make a soft creamy mix. Ripple in the lemon curd. Spoon a little mascarpone mixture into each tart case, then spoon over a few of the syrupy blueberries.

• Per tart 179 kcalories, protein 1g, carbohydrate 11g, fat 15g, saturated fat 7g, fibre 1g, added sugar 8g, salt 0.15g

The only rule with these tarts is to eat them straight from the oven while the centres are still gooey.

Warm chocolate and macadamia nut tarts

375g pack sweet pastry
200g/8oz dark chocolate, broken into pieces
2 tbsp double cream
1 tbsp Disaronno or brandy (optional)
2 large eggs, plus 1 yolk
50g/2oz caster sugar
85g/3oz macadamia nuts, chopped
icing sugar, to decorate

Takes 1 hour, plus chilling • Makes 4

1 Roll the pastry out to a £1 coin thickness then use to line four tartlet cases (about 10x3cm). Trim the excess then freeze for 30 minutes. Preheat the oven to 190°C/170°C fan/gas 5. Line the cases with parchment and baking beans, then cook on a baking sheet for 15 minutes. Remove the beans and paper, then cook for 3–5 minutes more until the pastry is pale golden and biscuity.
2 Melt the chocolate, cream and alcohol, if using, in a heatproof bowl over a pan of barely simmering water. Whisk the eggs, yolk and sugar until light and frothy. Briefly whisk the melted chocolate into the eggs and fold through most of the chopped macadamia nuts.
3 Fill the cases with the chocolate mix, scatter with the remaining nuts then bake for 12 minutes. The tops of the tarts will soufflé up and they should still be soft in the middle. Serve straight away, dusted with icing sugar.

• Per tart 867 kcalories, protein 12g, carbohydrate 77g, fat 59g, saturated fat 18g, fibre 4g, sugar 53g, salt 0.5g

Cute and easy to make, these little fruity buns
are sure to please at Easter time.

Hot cross muffin buns

450g/1lb strong white bread flour,
plus extra for dusting
50g/2oz cold butter, cut into pieces
7g sachet fast-action yeast
2 tsp ground mixed spice
50g/2oz golden caster sugar
finely grated zest of 1 lemon
250ml/9fl oz milk, tepid,
plus extra to glaze
2 large eggs, beaten
200g/8oz luxury mixed dried fruit,
cherries halved

FOR THE CROSSES AND GLAZE
2 tbsp plain flour
5–6 tsp cold water
golden syrup, to glaze

Takes about 3 hours • Makes 9

1 Put the flour and ½ teaspoon of salt in a
bowl, and rub in the butter. Stir in the yeast,
mixed spice, sugar and lemon zest, then mix
in the milk and eggs. Knead for 10 minutes,
then leave to rise, covered, until doubled in
size, for about 1 hour.
2 Pat into a large flat circle on a lightly floured
surface then tip the fruit into the middle and
encase it in the dough. Knead the fruit in
evenly, then shape into nine balls.
3 Cut nine 14cm squares of baking
parchment and use to line a muffin tin. Drop
in balls of dough. Cover with oiled cling film,
then leave for 30–45 minutes or until doubled
in size. Preheat the oven to 200°C/180°C
fan/gas 6.
4 Brush the buns with milk. Mix the flour and
water, then pipe as crosses over the buns.
Bake for 15 minutes or until golden. Brush
with golden syrup while warm.

• Per bun 352 kcalories, protein 10g, carbohydrate 65g, fat
8g, saturated fat 4g, fibre 2g, added sugar 8g, salt 0.54g

Just a handful of ingredients make a deliciously
easy twist on apple pie.

Blackberry and apple pasties

icing sugar, to dust
425g pack ready-rolled
shortcrust pastry
2 Bramley apples, peeled,
cored and chopped
2 tbsp light brown soft sugar
150g punnet blackberries
thick cream, to serve

Takes 35 minutes • Makes 4

1 Preheat the oven to 200°C/180°C fan/
gas 6. Dust a work surface with icing sugar,
then unroll the pastry and cut out four rounds
using a small side plate as a template.
2 Combine the apples and sugar with the
blackberries, and put a small pile on each
pastry circle. Dampen the edge of the pastry,
then fold over to encase the fruit. Pinch and
fold over the pastry along one edge to make
a pasty shape. Slash each pasty three times,
lift on to a baking sheet and bake for around
20 minutes or until puffed and golden. Serve
with cream.

• Per pasty 471 kcalories, protein 7g, carbohydrate
58g, fat 25g, saturated fat 10g, fibre 3g, sugar 20g,
salt 0.85g

Deliciously golden, light doughnuts and not a deep-fryer in sight.

Hot sugared doughnuts

250g/9oz plain flour, plus
extra for kneading
½ × 7g sachet fast-action yeast
50g/2oz golden caster sugar, plus
50g/2oz extra for coating
2 large egg yolks
150ml/¼ pint milk, warmed
50g/2oz butter, melted, plus 50g/2oz
extra for coating
370g jar raspberry jam

Takes 45 minutes, plus rising
and cooling • Makes 20

1 Mix the flour, yeast, sugar and ½ teaspoon of salt in a large bowl. Beat the yolks, milk and butter together, and stir into the flour mix to make a dough. Leave to stand for 10 minutes.
2 Lightly flour a work surface then knead the dough for about 5 minutes until smooth and springy. Leave to rise in an oiled, covered bowl in a warm place for about 2 hours.
3 Knead once or twice then shape into walnut-sized balls and put on baking sheets, well spaced. Cover again, then leave to rise for 30 minutes–1 hour until risen and pillowy. Preheat the oven to 190°C/170°C fan/gas 5.
4 Bake for 12–15 minutes until risen and dark golden. Melt the extra butter in a pan and put the extra sugar into a large bowl. Cool the doughnuts for a few minutes, then brush with the melted butter and roll in sugar. Pipe in jam using a 5mm nozzle or serve warm with jam for dipping.

• Per doughnut 135 kcalories, protein 2g, carbohydrate 18g, fat 7g, saturated fat 3g, fibre none, sugar 8g, salt 0.21g

Light and puffy, Devonshire splits are the ultimate nostalgic teatime treat. Enjoy this easy recipe with strawberry jam and clotted cream.

Devonshire splits

600g/1lb 5oz strong white bread flour, plus extra for dusting
50g/2oz butter at room temperature, cut into pieces
7g sachet fast-action yeast
2 tsp caster sugar
400ml/14fl oz full-fat milk, warmed
strawberry jam
2 × 113g pots clotted cream
icing sugar, for dusting

Takes 45 minutes, plus rising
Makes 12

1 Put the flour and butter in a large bowl and rub into fine crumbs. Stir in the yeast, 1 teaspoon of salt and the sugar. Stir in the milk to make a soft dough. Knead on a floured surface for 10 minutes; sprinkle with flour if it sticks. Put the dough in a large buttered bowl and cover with cling film. Leave in a warm place for 50 minutes–1 hour.

2 Knead briefly, then cut into twelve even pieces. Keep the dough covered as you shape the rolls into rounds. Put on to two greased baking sheets.

3 Cover again then leave to rise for 40–50 minutes, depending on the room temperature. Meanwhile, preheat the oven to 220°C/200°C fan/gas 7.

4 Bake for 15–20 minutes until pale golden. Cool on a wire rack. When cold, cut at an angle with a serrated knife. Spread with jam and clotted cream and dust with icing sugar.

• Per split 366 kcalories, protein 7g, carbohydrate 48g, fat 17g, saturated fat 11g, fibre 2g, added sugar 8g, salt 0.56g

These are so quick, plus you get all the different textures and flavours in each mouthful. If using bought mincemeat, you can customize to suit your taste by adding your favourite nuts and dried fruit.

Mincemeat custard pies

2 × 150g pots Devon custard
6 level tbsp ground almonds
375g pack ready-rolled puff pastry
16–18 tsp mincemeat (about a 410g jar)
flaked almonds, for scattering
icing sugar, for dusting

Takes 20 minutes • Makes 16–18

1 Preheat the oven to 220°C/200°C fan/gas 7. Stir the custard and almonds together.
2 Unroll the pastry, then cut out circles using a 7cm plain round cutter. Gather up the pastry trimmings, re-roll, then cut out more circles – you should get sixteen to eighteen. Use to line a couple of muffin tins.
3 Spoon a heaped teaspoon of the custard mix into each tart case, then top with a scant teaspoon of mincemeat. Scatter over some flaked almonds, then bake for 10 minutes until puffy and golden. Cool briefly in the tin, then dust with icing sugar and serve still slightly warm.

• Per pie (16) 169 kcalories, protein 4g, carbohydrate 16g, fat 11g, saturated fat 3g, fibre 1g, sugar 7g, salt 0.22g

These make a great present or a sweet little something for the children to take around to neighbours at Christmas time.

Stollen buns

500g/1lb 2oz strong white bread flour, plus extra for dusting
3 tbsp light muscovado sugar
7g sachet fast-action yeast
3 tsp ground mixed spice
1 tsp salt
85g/3oz butter
200ml/7fl oz milk, plus 1 tbsp to glaze
1 tbsp black treacle
2 tbsp brandy
2 large eggs
2 tbsp sunflower or vegetable oil
250g mix sultanas, raisins, peel and chopped glacé cherries
zest of 1 orange and 1 lemon
400g/14oz white marzipan
a handful of flaked almonds

FOR THE SYRUP
50g/2oz icing sugar mixed with
4 tbsp hot water

Takes 1 hour, plus rising • Makes 14

1 Mix the first five ingredients in a large bowl. Rub in the butter. Warm the milk, treacle and brandy, then beat in one egg and the oil, and mix into the bowl. Set aside for 10 minutes, then briefly knead on a floured surface. Cover and leave to rise until doubled in size.
2 Roll the dough to A4 size. Scatter over the dried fruit and zests, then knead until even. Roll to about 50x15cm. Dampen the edges. Roll the marzipan to a 50cm sausage, then roll the dough around it. Pinch to seal.
3 Preheat the oven to 200°C/180°C fan/gas 6. Slice the dough into 14, discarding the very ends. Flatten a little, then put on to lined baking sheets, well spaced. Re-cover and rise until pillowy. Beat the remaining egg with the 1 tablespoon of milk and use to glaze. Sprinkle with almonds. Bake for 15 minutes. Generously brush the syrup over the buns.

• Per bun 407 kcalories, protein 8g, carbohydrate 68g, fat 13g, saturated fat 4g, fibre 2g, sugar 41g, salt 0.55g

The pastry for these pies is very unusual and completely delicious. Made with cream cheese, it's light, crumbly and doesn't need rolling out.

Pecan tassies

85g/3oz pecan nuts, toasted
1 egg yolk
50g/2oz light brown soft sugar
2 tbsp maple syrup
½ tsp vanilla extract
15g/½oz butter, melted
cream and maple syrup, to serve

FOR THE PASTRY
50g/2oz pecan nuts
50g/2oz full-fat soft cheese
50g/2oz butter, softened
50g/2oz plain flour, plus
extra for dusting

Takes 40 minutes, plus cooling
Makes 12

1 For the pastry, whiz the pecans in a food processor until finely ground then pulse in the remaining ingredients with a pinch of salt just until the dough comes together. Lightly flour your hands, then roll the dough into twelve small balls. Use your fingers to gently press them into the bottom and up the sides of a 12-hole mini-muffin tin. Chill for 10 minutes.
2 Preheat the oven to 180°C/160°C fan/ gas 4. Reserve twelve toasted pecans then roughly chop the rest. Whisk together the remaining ingredients with a pinch of salt. Stir in the chopped pecans.
3 Bake the cases for 5 minutes – gently press down with a teaspoon if the pastry puffs up a little. Spoon 1–2 teaspoons of filling into each case and top with a whole pecan. Bake for 15–20 minutes until golden and set. Cool a little in the tin then eat warm with cream and maple syrup.

• Per bun 173 kcalories, protein 2g, carbohydrate 10g, fat 14g, saturated fat 4g, fibre 1g, sugar 7g, salt 0.13g

Apple strudel is served for afternoon tea all over Germany and Austria. Go on, try these with a cup of coffee and a dollop of cream.

Spiced apple filo parcels

3 dessert apples, peeled, cored and finely chopped
zest and juice ½ lemon
50g/2oz sultanas
1 tbsp light muscovado sugar
½ tsp ground mixed spice
6 large sheets filo pastry, about 48x30cm
40g/1½oz butter, melted
sesame seeds, for sprinkling

Takes 40 minutes, plus cooling
Makes 6

1 Preheat the oven to 200°C/180°C fan/ gas 6. Put the apples, lemon zest and juice, sultanas, sugar and spice in a frying pan. Cook covered on a low heat for 8–10 minutes until apples are tender. Cool slightly.
2 Lightly brush a sheet of pastry with butter (keep spare pastry covered). Fold lengthways into three, making one long piece.
Put a spoonful of the mixture 4cm from the top short edge. Fold top left corner to the right, making a triangle over the filling. Keep folding into a parcel. Repeat with the remaining pastry and filling.
3 Put the parcels on a lightly greased baking sheet; brush with a little butter. Sprinkle over a few sesame seeds and bake for around 15 minutes or until golden. Serve warm.

• Per parcel 246 kcalories, protein 4g, carbohydrate 42g, fat 8g, saturated fat 4g, fibre 2g, added sugar 4g, salt 1.17g

This recipe makes four dessert-size portions, but you could easily make eight small tarts for tea instead. Just give them a few minutes less in the oven.

Rhubarb crumble puffs

5 rhubarb sticks, cut into 3cm pieces
1 tsp ground cinnamon
3 tbsp plain flour, plus extra for dusting
5 tbsp brown soft sugar
½ × 500g block puff pastry
3 tbsp unsalted butter
50g/2oz rolled oats

Takes 30–35 minutes • Makes 4

1 Preheat the oven to 200°C/180°C fan/gas 6. In a bowl, toss the rhubarb with cinnamon, 1 tablespoon of the flour and 2 tablespoons of the sugar. Line a baking sheet with baking parchment. Roll out the pastry on a floured surface to about 20x30cm, then cut into quarters and put on the sheet.
2 Rub together the remaining flour and sugar, the butter and oats to make a rough crumble mixture. Divide the rhubarb among the pastry quarters, leaving a 1cm rim. Sprinkle the oat mixture over, then fold and pinch each corner to keep the filling in. Bake for 20–25 minutes, then serve warm.

• Per puff 465 kcalories, protein 6g, carbohydrate 53g, fat 27g, saturated fat 13g, fibre 3g, sugar 21g, salt 0.57g

Index

SPECIAL TRIAL OFFER

3 issues of GoodFood magazine for £1

GoodFood magazine is a must for everyone who loves food and cooking. It's packed with over 100 seasonal recipes, tested by our experts so you can be sure they'll work first time and with recipes from all the top TV chefs, it's a feast in itself!

Subscribing is easy, simply

☎ Call **0844 848 3414**
quoting code GFRB1209 (lines open Mon-Fri 8am-8pm, Saturday 9am-1pm)

🖱 Visit **www.subscribeonline.co.uk/goodfood**
and quote code GFRB1209